D0556539

A GUIDE TO THE
Sequoia Groves of California

A GUIDE TO THE
Sequoia
Groves
of California

By Dwight Willard

YOSEMITE ASSOCIATION
YOSEMITE NATIONAL PARK, CALIFORNIA

Acknowledgments

I am deeply grateful to Joseph Engbeck, Jr., for acting as photo editor, and for much other help without which this book would not have reached print. Thanks also to Wendell Flint and Robert Rogers for their helpful reviews of the initial manuscript of the book.

Yosemite Association
Box 545
Yosemite National Park
California 95389

The **Yosemite Association** initiates and supports interpretive, educational, research, scientific, and environmental programs in Yosemite National Park, in cooperation with the National Park Service. Authorized by Congress, the Association provides services and direct financial support in order to promote park stewardship and enrich the visitor experience.

   To learn more about our activities and other publications, or for information about membership, please write to the address above or call (209) 379-2646.

   Visit the Yosemite Association web site at: http://yosemite.org

Library of Congress Cataloging-in-Publication Data

Willard, Dwight.
   A guide to the sequoia groves of California / by Dwight Willard.
      p.cm
   ISBN 0-939666-81-2
      1. Giant sequoia–California. 2. Parks–California–Guidebooks. 3. California–Guidebooks. I. Title: Sequoia groves of California. II. Yosemite Association. III. Title.

   SD397.G52 W543 2000
   634.9'758'09794–dc21
                                        00-031944

Maps by Eureka Cartography, Berkeley, California.
Project coordination by Joseph H. Engbeck, Jr.
Design by Robin Weiss Design, San Carlos, California.
Front cover photograph by Jeff Grandy.
Back cover photograph by Dwight Willard.

Printed in Singapore.

Contents

Preface   6

How to Use This Book   9

Groves North of the Kings River   13
The Euro-American Discovery of Sequoias   19
The Tree-Naming Phenomenon   23

Groves in the Southern Kings River Watershed   29
Attitudes About Logged Sequoia Groves   34
The Age of Sequoias   45
The Emotional Response to Sequoias   51

Groves in or Contiguous to the Kaweah River Watershed   59
Grove Managers   65
Grove Distribution   73
Giant Sequoia and Coast Redwood Compared   83

Groves in the Tule River Watershed   87
The Size of the Sequoias   98

Other Southern Sierra Groves   103
The Future of the Sequoias   107

USGS Topographical Maps with Giant Sequoia Groves   110
Public Agency Information Sources   112
Sequoia Grove Access Guide   113
Selected Bibliography   119
Photo Credits   120
Index   121

Maps

California Sequoia Grove Map Index   8
Groves North of the Kings River   12
Groves in the Southern Kings River Watershed   28
Groves in or Contiguous to the Kaweah River Watershed   58
Distribution of Sequoia Groves in California   73
Groves in the Tule River Watershed   86
Other Southern Sierra Groves   102

Giant sequoias are world famous for their size, beauty, and longevity. Yet most giant sequoia groves are little known and seldom visited. The main purpose of this book is to provide a convenient introduction to all of the natural sequoia groves of the Sierra Nevada. I hope this book will encourage visits to the lesser known groves, and increase appreciation of them.

Hundreds of thousands of people see the giant sequoias in the Sierra Nevada each year, but most experience these great trees in just a few places: the North Calaveras Grove in Calaveras Big Trees State Park, the Mariposa Grove in Yosemite National Park, the Grant Grove in Kings Canyon National Park, and Giant Forest in Sequoia National Park. These are the best known groves, but they are only a small part of the overall sequoia resource. Some of the lesser known groves in Sequoia National Park and Sequoia National Forest also have major sequoia attractions, including individual trees that are comparable to famous trees in the most visited groves.

Most people are surprised to learn that there are more sequoia groves in Sequoia National Forest than there are in the national parks. Some of these unpublicized national forest groves include expansive and spectacular sequoia resources. Freeman Creek Grove is the largest unlogged grove on national forest land. Black Mountain Grove, McIntyre Grove, and Evans Grove are also quite large and have plentiful old growth sequoias.

In global terms, natural sequoia groves are rare. Sequoias naturally grow only in the Sierra Nevada, on a total of 36,000 to 38,000 acres (depending on how grove boundaries are defined). This is equivalent to less than one-third of the surface area of Lake Tahoe. In contrast, coast redwoods occur naturally on nearly two million acres. Unlogged natural sequoia forest is even more rare, covering less than 25,000 acres. Though they dominate the scene where they occur, the very largest size category of sequoias—those exceeding twenty feet in diameter at breast height—are a tiny percentage of the overall sequoia resource. There are fewer than 1,000 such trees in the universe. Yet it is not difficult for a visitor to "discover" such rare wonders in solitude, off the beaten track in the lesser known groves.

I have tried to point out the diverse character of the sequoia groves. Individual giant sequoias are similar from grove to grove, but the groves vary in terrain, forest condition, and scenic context. Some are purely old growth ecosystems, while others have varying forest conditions. Some groves are laced with creeks, while others lack any reliable surface water. Some groves surround the visitor in towering, thick forest, while in other groves, one can see over sequoia crowns to deep canyons or up to high peaks. Some groves bear the marks of logging, paved roads and developed visitor facilities. But many groves are unmarked by human activity and remain wilderness.

Most sequoia groves are accessible by some type of road, but only a few, such as North Calaveras Grove and Giant Forest, can be reached by all-season paved roads. Access to many of the other groves is relatively difficult. Most roads that go to groves are forest service seasonal dirt roads. Such road access is subject to variable conditions, depending on weather and maintenance.

Only a few groves have extensive trail systems. Most have no trails at all, though closed dirt roads serve as trails in some areas. Some large groves with good road access, like Redwood Mountain Grove and McIntyre Grove, still have sections in wilderness condition. If you are considering a visit to a grove area that is accessible only by dirt road, trail, or cross-country route, you should check current conditions with the managing agency.

This book also seeks to expand awareness and appreciation of the resources and attractions of formerly logged groves. Almost all of the logged groves include some fine old growth trees that survived the logging. Mountain Home Grove, Evans Grove, and Black Mountain Grove, for example, all suffered substantial logging operations, but they nonetheless retain a multitude of old growth sequoias. Sequoia stumps and logs that remain from early logging can be quite interesting. For example, in addition to their impressive size, the stumps of old sequoias clearly reveal the extraordinary longevity of these trees, with sometimes thousands of years of exposed growth rings. Many formerly logged sequoia grove areas have impressive forest regrowth. The "young" forest in such groves often includes sequoias over seventy-five years old, and more than three feet in diameter. Some formerly logged grove areas are in the process of regaining old growth forest characteristics, though, of course, it will take millennia to produce giants comparable to some that were logged.

I have also tried to highlight other attractions that can be found in the sequoia groves. Notably, some groves have among the finest mixed conifer forest of pine, fir, and incense cedar that can be found in the Sierra Nevada. Groves also provide needed habitat for the spotted owl and other old growth dependent wildlife species.

Until the Giant Sequoia National Monument was created in April 2000, preservation of the groves in the national forests depended entirely upon U.S. Forest Service planning processes. There was no legal mandate for sequoia protection in the national forests as there was in the national parks. As a result, commercial logging occurred in some sequoia groves in Sequoia National Forest as recently as the 1980s. Those groves are now protected from commercial logging by the new monument designation, but an interested and informed public is still essential to their preservation and restoration over the long term. This book aims to promote the public interest in sequoias that is needed to help assure their best management and protection.

I hope this book will encourage more public enjoyment of the groves, and particularly of the lesser known groves. John Muir once advised readers to "climb the mountains and get their good tidings." The giant sequoias of the Sierra Nevada, in all of their beauty, diversity, and vitality, offer pure and ever-available good tidings.

DWIGHT WILLARD
May 2000

CALIFORNIA SEQUOIA GROVE
MAP INDEX

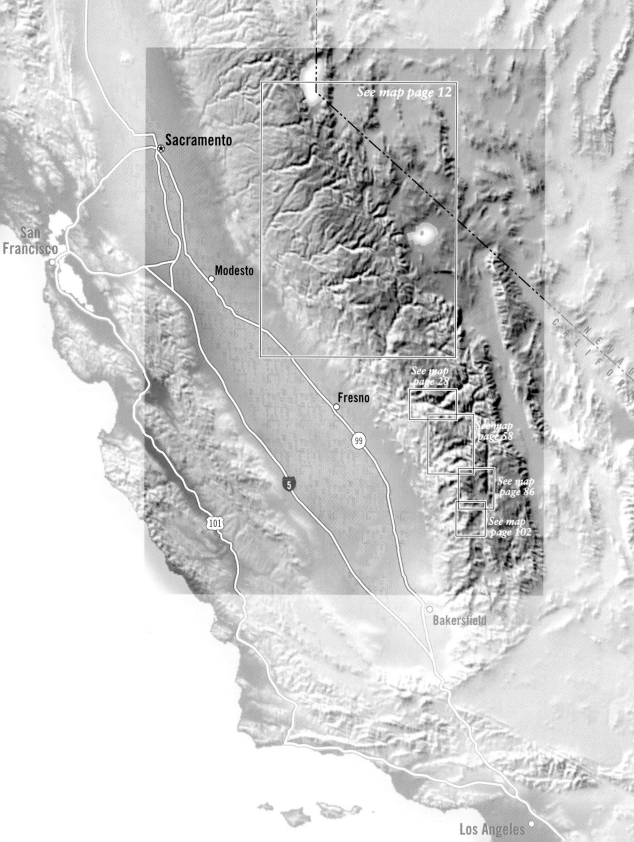

See map page 12

Sacramento

San Francisco

Modesto

Fresno

See map page 28

See map page 58

See map page 86

See map page 102

Bakersfield

Los Angeles

99

5

101

NEVADA

CALIFORNIA

This book divides the sixty-seven sequoia groves in California into five geographical sections. For each section a map is provided that shows the locations of the groves in that region. A brief summary detailing size, condition, manager, and access is included for each grove (see the explanatory notes below), followed by a longer narrative with additional information such as general description, historical facts, significance, notable trees, overall quality, and management notes.

Several short discussions of various aspects of the giant sequoias generally (their age, size, and distribution, for example) are sprinkled throughout the volume, and photographs of the groves accompany their descriptions.

Added at the end of the book are a list of the groves indicating the U.S. Geological Survey topographical maps on which they appear, and a list of public agencies and other entities responsible for managing the sequoia groves, with addresses, phone numbers, and web sites. A sequoia grove access guide and a selected bibliography complete the volume.

Explanation of Terms Used

The following information explains the terms used in the summary section at the start of each grove description.

Size

The different sequoia groves have been classified by size as follows:

Large: Groves over 600 acres;
Mid-size: Groves from 150 to 600 acres;
Small: Groves from 10 to 150 acres; and
Tiny: Very small groves, 10 acres or less.

Grove sizes are approximate and represent the total area within the grove perimeter defined by the outermost trees. Because some groves are a mosaic of areas with and without sequoias, the acreage where sequoias actually occur may be less than the described total grove area.

Condition

Sequoia resource conditions can be grouped into the following general categories:

Old growth: No significant sequoia logging has occurred.
    In old growth groves, natural mortality has occurred and rela-

tively young sequoias may be very common because of the effects of fire, other natural causes, and terrain. Logging of non-sequoia conifers may have taken place, so not all species can be characterized as "old growth."

Wilderness old growth: An old growth grove in a wilderness context.

For this book, wilderness is defined as a roadless area, accessible only on foot, in a wild, natural condition without human development or visitor facilities. These "wilderness" grove areas are usually not part of the legislated National Wilderness System. The "wilderness" groves described here are in national parks or remote national forest areas. They should retain their wilderness quality under present management plans.

Mixed: The common grove condition where much of the old growth sequoia resource survives, but where significant sequoia logging has taken place.

In some areas, this describes surviving giants and old growth trees in logged areas, while in others the logged and unlogged areas are distinct. Some "partially old growth" or "partially logged" groves retain unlogged areas equivalent in size to a large or medium-sized "old growth" grove.

Logged: Groves where sequoias were pervasively logged.

These grove areas are usually dominated by young conifers, including sequoias. In the case of groves logged from 70 to 110 years ago, the "young" sequoias which regenerated after logging now often stand over 100 feet tall and can be 3 to 6 feet in diameter (at breast height). So a "logged grove," or a logged area within a grove, may have recovered the character of continuous forest of large trees.

Manager

The entity responsible for management of each grove (most commonly the U.S. Forest Service or the U.S. National Park Service) is listed. More than 90 percent of the groves is in some form of public ownership. By contacting these managers, one can obtain additional information, particularly about current road and trail conditions (see page 112).

Access

Primary access information is provided to give an indication of the relative ease with which a grove can be visited:

Paved road: The grove can be easily reached on a paved road.

Relatively few of the groves can be reached in this way. Remember that all mountain roads are subject to weather-related closures and restrictions, particularly in winter.

Dirt road: Currently, the grove can be reached by driveable, unpaved road, but road conditions can be expected to be more varied and difficult, and very often inappropriate for passenger cars.

Dirt roads often have a long closure period regardless of weather; it is not unusual for such roads to be closed from the first heavy autumn snow through May. Most are in areas remote from services. Conditions can change suddenly in adverse weather. Many dirt roads (especially in Sequoia National Forest) have become undrivable due to lack of maintenance. *Always* check with the managing agency on the condition of dirt roads before trying to drive on them.

Trail: There is a currently-maintained trail or a closed road.

Cross-country: No road or trail access; a preferred access route may be lacking.

"Cross-country" access should be considered difficult and appropriate for only adventurous and skilled hikers. Route distance and difficulty vary from grove to grove. In some cases, traces of abandoned or unofficial trails exist on cross-country routes, but these can't be depended upon. Vegetation can rapidly obscure unmaintained trails.

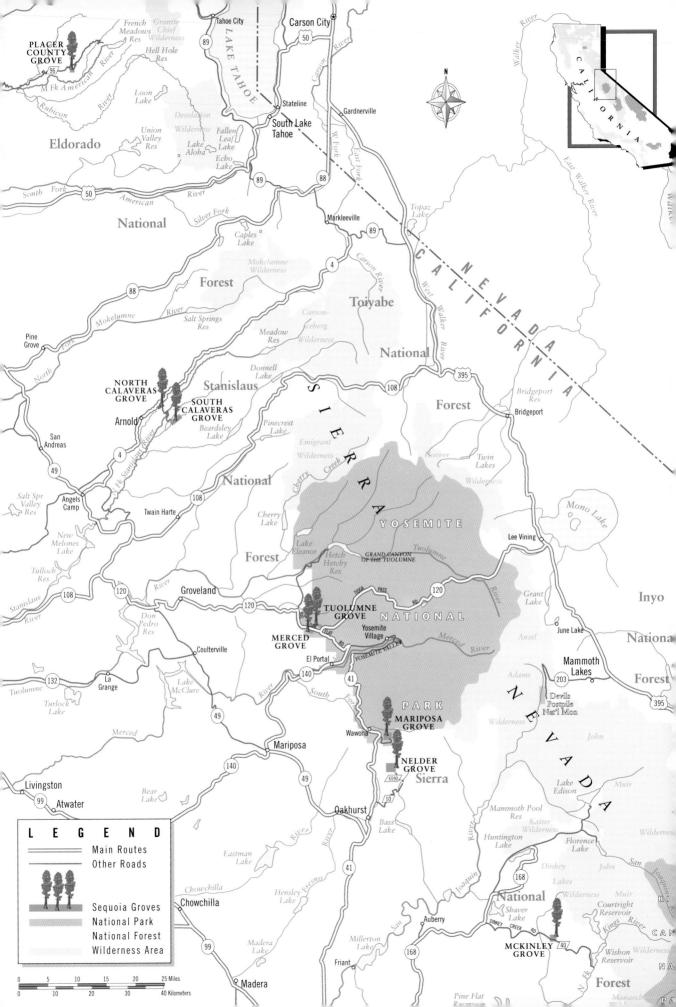

GROVES NORTH OF THE KINGS RIVER

PLACER COUNTY GROVE 15

NORTH CALAVERAS GROVE 15

SOUTH CALAVERAS GROVE 17

TUOLUMNE AND MERCED GROVES 18

MARIPOSA GROVE 20

NELDER GROVE 25

MCKINLEY GROVE 27

PLACER COUNTY GROVE

Size: Tiny
Condition: Old growth
Manager: Tahoe National Forest
Access: Paved road

This is the northernmost and smallest of all the sequoia groves. It is located in the American River watershed of Tahoe National Forest. It is also the farthest removed from other groves (about 60 miles from the North Calaveras Grove). The grove contains six living and two fallen sequoias, all within a few hundred feet of one another. Only two of the living trees and the two fallen sequoia logs are of "giant" size.

The grove illustrates that even very small sequoia groves can serve as fine old growth, mixed conifer reserves. Set within an unlogged 160-acre botanical preserve, it features an old growth forest with impressive specimens of sugar and ponderosa pine, incense cedar, and Douglas fir (the last of which occurs only in the northern groves). A short loop hike through this grove reveals the varied and impressive forest resources protected here, and provides a marked contrast to the surrounding forest that has long been managed for timber.

The Placer County Grove is a good example of a small grove, with good road access, offering visitors an undeveloped, beautifully natural forest just a short hike from grove-edge parking.

NORTH CALAVERAS GROVE

Size: Small
Condition: Old growth
Manager: Calaveras Big Trees State Park
Access: Paved road

The small, heavily-touristed North Calaveras Grove, just off Highway 4 in Calaveras Big Trees State Park, is the easiest grove to reach from the San Francisco Bay Area. Discovered by a pioneer in 1850, it was the first grove to be widely publicized and developed for tourism; a hotel (later destroyed by fire) was built in the grove by 1854. The North Calaveras Grove has been described as the oldest continuously-used recreation site in the western United States.

Though the grove has long been impacted by humans, it has a beautiful, unspoiled appearance. State park management has carefully shielded most of the grove from development impacts, and has conducted prescribed burning with great care to preserve scenic quality. The grove is a treat to visit in all seasons, and is a perfect introduction to California's sequoia groves. A range of sights, from living specimens to huge fallen logs and spectacular snags, from creekside and hillside trees to inspiring old growth mammoths, can

Mother of the Forest, North Calaveras Grove.

Pioneer Cabin Tree, North Calaveras Grove.

be appreciated from the short, nearly-level loop trail.

The grove is a dense stand of about sixty acres, with more than one hundred sequoias measuring over five feet in diameter (at breast height), including about seventy-five with diameters over ten feet. These large trees are mixed with younger sequoias and a fine old growth, mixed-conifer forest. The towering pines and firs distinguish this small preserve that sits surrounded by thousands of acres of prime Sierra Nevada forest land that has been logged of its old growth. Mature and stately pines, firs, and incense cedars once blanketed the fertile mid-elevation slopes of the northern Sierra, which slopes have been transformed by commercial timber production into a forest mosaic dominated by younger stands.

Unfortunately, the only mature sequoias ever cut in the grove were its two largest specimens. They were felled in the early 1850s for exhibition displays. The present Big Stump is the remnant of the "Discovery Tree," which has the biggest base diameter of any grove specimen. The Mother of the Forest, which almost certainly was the grove's largest tree in total volume, died a lingering death after more than a hundred feet of its bark was stripped for exhibition display. The present, shortened snag is what remains after early twentieth-century fires. The Empire State Tree is now the grove's largest living tree in overall volume.

The North Calaveras Grove has its own tunnel tree, cut by pioneers in the 1880s. This Pioneer Cabin Tree has the greatest basal diameter of any living grove tree. When Yosemite's tunneled Wawona Tree fell in 1969, the Pioneer Cabin Tree became the largest of the several living tunneled sequoias.

SOUTH CALAVERAS GROVE

Size: Mid-size
Condition: Wilderness old growth
Manager: Calaveras Big Trees State Park
Access: Trail

The South Calaveras Grove, located in a wilderness section of Calaveras Big Trees State Park accessible only by trail, is one of the Sierra's most spectacular old growth groves. Covering about 450 acres, it is the largest of the eight groves north of the Kings River. The sequoias fill the bottom of the valley of Big Trees Creek, a tributary of the North Fork of the Stanislaus River. The grove's entire watershed is protected by state park status. Until the creation of Giant Sequoia National Monument in April 2000, such grove watershed protection was uncommon outside of the national parks.

The grove terrain is fairly gentle, and the forest is relatively open due to its old growth character and the effect of controlled fires. This makes it an ideal setting for leisurely and meandering grove explorations. The lower section of the grove features a loop trail, while the upper section is trail-less.

Like the North Calaveras Grove a few miles away, the South Calaveras is famous for its magnificent old growth, mixed conifers, as well as for its sequoias. Conservationist Frederick Law Olmsted, Jr., concluded in the 1940s that the grove and its neighboring old growth areas (some of which were later logged) had the most impressive sugar pine stands in the Sierra Nevada, particularly because of the "prevalence" of very large-sized specimens. Threatened logging of the grove's abundant large pines and firs spurred the State of California to acquire the grove in the 1950s.

Both here and in the North Calaveras Grove, controlled fire has been used to restore natural understory conditions and reduce the risk of catastrophic fire. Many regard the fire management practiced at the Calaveras Groves to be a model for controlled burns in sequoia groves. Techniques include the careful application of light-intensity fires, and the pre-fire clearance of downed wood and saplings from around the base of sequoias so that they won't be scorched or damaged. This type of burning causes no enduring or controversial scenic blight.

On the other hand, some critics of the Calaveras burn program believe that the fires used are not adequately intense from an ecological perspective. More severe, "hotter" prescribed fires have been conducted in Giant Forest in Sequoia National Park, and comparisons of the long-term effects of different burning techniques in those two groves should prove interesting. Through its fire program, the South Calaveras Grove has maintained a relatively open forest understory, in marked contrast to the unnaturally overgrown understory conditions in many grove areas where fire has been excluded for many decades.

The grove has more than one thousand large sequoias, of which at least four hundred are ten feet in diameter or larger (at breast height). With many of the oldest age-class trees, the grove offers the visitor multiple huge specimens, displayed as scattered individuals

Palace Hotel Tree, South Calaveras Grove.

and in striking pairs, trios, and larger clusters.

The trailside Agassiz Tree, with an enormous, hollow base and fire scar, is the grove's largest. The Old Goliath in the upper grove was one of the largest standing sequoias before it toppled in the 1860s. Its spectacular log is one of the many wonders to be discovered by heading off the beaten path in this remarkable grove.

TUOLUMNE AND MERCED GROVES

Size: Small
Condition: Old growth
Manager: Yosemite National Park
Access: Tuolumne: Closed paved road; Merced: Trail (closed dirt road)

Though relatively small, the Tuolumne and Merced Groves in Yosemite National Park are superb sequoia attractions. The nearby groves have closely grouped giants, set in some of the nicest old growth mixed conifer forest remaining anywhere in the Sierra Nevada (including notable sugar pine specimens). The Tuolumne Grove is surrounded by extensive old growth forest, some of which was added to Yosemite as late as the early 1930s after being threatened with logging. In contrast, the Merced Grove is an example of a small old growth preserve surrounded by lands logged in the early twentieth century. The groves themselves escaped significant logging; narrow road construction was the only logging impact. Their old growth sequoias all survive. Neither grove has public facilities.

The trees in one of these groves were almost certainly the first sequoias described by Euro-American explorers; Zenas Leonard, a member of the 1833 Joseph Walker party that crossed through the Yosemite area, described seeing "trees of the Redwood species, incredibly large."

The Tuolumne Grove is in the drainage of North Crane Creek, just north of the intersection of the Big Oak Flat and Tioga Roads. The grove is bisected by a paved, narrow road that has been indefinitely closed to vehicles. It has about twenty-five living sequoias over five feet in diameter (at breast height), including at least fifteen that are over ten feet in diameter, as well as numerous smaller sequoias, spread over about twenty-five acres.

The Siamese Twins are a spectacular pair of very tall specimens with a fused base more than sixteen feet in diameter (at breast height). The King of the Forest, with a base circumference of over 103 feet, has by far the largest base of any living tree in the grove, though it has lost most of its bark and trunk to fire. The most famous specimen is the Dead Giant, a huge, broken-off snag (base diameter 29.5 feet,) which was tunnelled by pioneers in 1878, when the grove was on the then main route to Yosemite, the old Big Oak Flat Road. Though nearly at the northern limit of the present sequoia range, these giants in their prime condition probably compared favorably in size with the southern Sierra giants that now dominate lists of the "largest" sequoias.

Merced Grove.

The Tuolumne Grove is considered by many to be another of the ideal models of controlled burn implementation. It did not suffer the controversial intense fire effects which occurred in some Sequoia National Park controlled burns.

The Merced Grove is in the small valley of Moss Creek, accessible by short hike west from the Big Oak Flat Road (Highway 120). The grove is bisected by the unpaved Coulterville Road to Yosemite (constructed in the 1870s) that is no longer open to public vehicle use. Ironically, the grove almost certainly saw more tourists in the late nineteenth century (when it was on a major Yosemite access route) than it does today. It has about forty sequoias over five feet in diameter, including about fifteen specimens over ten feet in diameter (at breast height), in addition to numerous younger sequoias, spread over about twenty acres.

Dead Giant, Tuolumne Grove.

THE EURO-AMERICAN DISCOVERY OF SEQUOIAS

Sequoias were not described by Euro-Americans until the 1839 published account by Zenas Leonard of his Sierra Nevada crossing with the Joseph Walker party in 1833. Leonard described "incredibly large" trees of the "redwood species." The Walker party's route is uncertain, but authorities have concluded that Leonard was describing the discovery of either the Tuolumne or Merced Grove in present Yosemite National Park. Leonard's published report was barely noticed.

The groves were first broadly publicized when several California journalists recounted the "discovery" of the North Calaveras Grove in 1852 by A. T. Dowd, who had been hunting. Within a few years, the still fantastic sounding stories of the sequoias were widely circulated in the United States and Europe, luring both loggers and curious tourists.

MARIPOSA GROVE

Size: Mid-size
Condition: Old growth
Manager: Yosemite National Park
Access: Paved road

Mariposa Grove.

The heavily-visited Mariposa Grove is one of the major attractions of Yosemite National Park. It is a fine, mid-sized, two-part, old growth grove. A two-mile paved spur road from the Wawona Road (Highway 41) provides easy, three-season, grove-edge access. It is one of only two groves with a visitor shuttle running through it (late spring through early fall) on a road closed to public vehicle use. There is a good trail network. Visitor facilities include a museum in the upper part of the grove. In winter, there are cross-country ski trails.

The grove has more than six hundred large sequoias, including about two hundred at least ten feet in diameter (at breast height), as well as hundreds of younger sequoias in old growth, mixed conifer forest. The sequoias are divided between a smaller lower section and a substantially larger, higher elevation part. Most of the Mariposa Grove is in the cooler, higher elevation phase of the mixed conifer forest dominated by white fir and sugar pine. This association with white firs and sugar pines is common in most of the sequoia's southern range.

The picturesque Grizzly Giant, in the lower part of the grove, is one of the most famous of all sequoias, with the grove's largest base perimeter (96.5 feet). It has a notable lean, which is rare for the largest sequoias. Such a lean produces a situation of awesome tonnage without vertical support, seasonally aggravated by snow weight. Nevertheless, the Grizzly is unlikely to fall soon, because its enormous base provides a securely low center of gravity. At breast height, the Grizzly's circumference is greater than that of the General Sherman Tree in Sequoia National Park. As is the case with many old growth sequoias, the trunk volume of the Grizzly Giant continues to grow rapidly. Comparison of measurements from the 1930s and the 1990s by Wendell Flint shows that the Grizzly gained an astonishing 11 percent in trunk volume in about sixty years.

Contrary to historical impressions of the Grizzly Giant's preeminence, the Washington Tree, in the upper grove, is the largest in total volume, slightly bigger than the Grizzly Giant. It is also the largest surviving sequoia in any grove north of the Kings River.

The Wawona Tree, often described as the most photographed tree in the world, was the most grand and famous of the several sequoia "tunnel trees." It fell in 1969 at the age of about 2,200 years. The tunnel carved through it in 1881 accommodated hundreds of stagecoaches and thousands of motor vehicles over the years. Though the tunnel pleased and fascinated visitors, it prematurely killed the tree by weakening its base. The Wawona was one of the largest trees in the Mariposa Grove. The smaller, tunneled California Tree still grows vigorously a short distance from the Grizzly Giant.

Another example of the impact of the human presence in the

Above: President Theodore Roosevelt with John Muir and others in the Mariposa Grove, 1903.

Left: Mariposa Grove Museum in the upper grove.

Left: Mariposa Grove.
Right: *Grizzly Giant.*

grove is the "Massachusetts Tree," once one of the grove's largest specimens. It fell in 1927, partially because of root damage caused by road construction in the 1870s.

Along with the North Calaveras Grove, the Mariposa Grove was one of the first to be discovered by pioneers and to be publicized and developed for tourists. Yosemite pioneer Galen Clark built a cabin in the grove in 1864. Some of the earliest photographs of sequoias were taken by C. L. Weed in the Mariposa Grove in 1859.

The Mariposa Grove was the first grove to receive legislative protection, when Congress granted the grove and Yosemite Valley to the State of California for public use and recreation in 1864. In 1906, the grove became part of greater Yosemite National Park.

In response to the early tourist boom, overnight facilities, known as the Big Trees Lodge, were built within the grove, but these were removed decades ago. Now the grove is open for day use only.

While it has not been commercially logged, the Mariposa Grove has the longest history of significant non-commercial vegetation management of any grove. During much of the first century of grove protection, a forest "housekeeping" mentality resulted in episodic "cleanups" (i.e. cutting and removal) of understory trees and brush, as well as some logging of larger pines and firs. In part of the grove, the forest was swept clear of all vegetation and forest litter beneath the mature conifers, as if it were a floor to be cleaned. This management approach, considered bizarre now, reflected a lack of understanding of the importance of preserving natural ecosystem processes.

More recently, ecologically-based controlled fire treatments,

The Mariposa Grove offers a good case study of the tree-naming (and renaming) phenomenon associated with every well-visited grove. By 1919, about 140 Mariposa Grove sequoias had names (and signs) that memorialized generals, politicians, and national and local celebrities, many of whom soon became unknown to the visiting public. These namings were unofficial, unsystematic, and often duplicative. About 1920, the National Park Service discontinued the practice of naming and signing trees, while perpetuating the use of well-recognized names for the most-noted specimens in popular groves.

The excessive tree-naming fad has passed. On the other hand, naming some giants reflects an almost instinctive, highly resonant human impulse to somehow distinguish each majestic sequoia specimen individually, and to have human connection with the sequoias' grandeur and seeming immortality. There is also a practical motivation. In the absence of names, it is hard to communicate about specific sequoias. Descriptions such as "the largest sequoia on the upper ridge in the northeast section of the grove" are too problematic. Often several nearby majestic specimens may be comparable in size and form, or hard to judge. If a giant loses its top, a description of "largest" may not even be an accurate description from one year to the next. So, in the modern era, even the most naturally respectful will maintain the practice of naming some trees.

Grizzly Giant.

intended to simulate the effects of natural fire, have replaced earlier management practices. The forest has regained its health despite the erratic past human impacts on the grove vegetation. The Mariposa Grove is especially valuable from the research perspective; its lengthy protected status and management by park professionals have resulted in very comprehensive documentation of its natural and human history.

NELDER GROVE

Size: Mid-size
Condition: Mixed
Manager: Sierra National Forest
Access: Dirt road

The Nelder Grove, four air miles south of the Mariposa Grove in the Sierra National Forest, is the only grove north of the Kings River to have suffered substantial logging. Access is by a rough seasonal dirt road, and there are a few short grove trails. There is a small campground.

John Muir visited the grove in 1875 and later unsuccessfully urged that it be added to Yosemite National Park. The ever-curious Muir's journal notes a fallen sugar pine in the grove that was 440 years old and 8 feet 3 inches in diameter (excluding the bark). The Nelder Grove was one of the prime sugar pine locations in the Sierra, as well as a trove of sequoias.

About 280 mature sequoias were logged between 1874 and 1892, along with much of the majestic sugar pine and mixed conifer old growth. The grove's naturally fallen sequoia logs were also largely harvested. Current forest service policy now prohibits commercial logging in the grove.

The Nelder Grove shows that "logged" groves are still major sequoia resources, which can recover many of their pre-logging natural values. While it is home to the enduring spectacle of the massive stumps of logged specimens, it retains many old growth sequoias. Like other groves that suffered substantial sequoia logging seventy-five or more years ago, the Nelder Grove also has seen the renewal of a vigorous forest of large mixed conifers and young sequoias that regenerated after logging. It is a highly scenic grove with about 108 surviving old growth sequoias, including about ninety over ten feet in diameter (at breast height), in four relatively scattered areas that total about three hundred acres. The largest concentration of old growth sequoias, about forty, is in the grove's Upper Nelder Creek/ Nelder Basin section.

Because during the sequoia logging of the nineteenth-century the primary Nelder Grove sawmill was not adapted to handling logs over six feet in diameter, the sequoias that the loggers spared were often the largest. This has created a pleasing, if misleading impres-

Bull Buck Tree.

Mariposa Grove.

Giant sequoias, living and dead.

sion, that all of the grove's old growth specimens are impressively big, rather than spanning a broader range of mature sizes.

One of the grove's largest specimens, the Forest King, was toppled in 1870 for exhibition purposes by the unusual technique of excavating soil and cutting the roots so that the tree falls from its own weight. This was the earliest known harvest of an old growth sequoia south of the Mariposa Grove.

In the pre-chain-saw era, cutting through the immense butt swell of an old growth sequoia was a considerable challenge. To hasten their work, the loggers made axe-chiseled notches well above the basal swell, mounted boards to stand on, then cut. The result was very high stumps. The Nelder Grove has more of these high stumps than any other grove area. The practice of cutting stumps "high" continued through the early twentieth century heyday of sequoia logging in groves like the Converse Basin.

As most of the Nelder Grove's sequoia logging occurred during the 1880s, the present stands of second growth sequoia there are among the oldest (a century or more) and finest of any logged grove area. Many tall, young sequoias have diameters of four to six feet. If protected, these trees can regain old growth characteristics in another half-century, though it would take closer to a millennium to achieve the sizes of the lost giants.

The Nelder Tree, in Nelder Basin, is the grove's largest survivor in total volume (approximately 35,000 cubic feet). It is second in total size only to the Washington Tree of the Mariposa Grove among sequoias north of the Kings River.

The grove's second largest sequoia, the Bull Buck, attracted notoriety in the 1970s as a possible challenger for the title of world's biggest tree because of its huge flared base. Precise measurements confirmed that it was far smaller than the title-holding General Sherman Tree. But the Bull Buck is a rapidly growing specimen that, if protected, might conceivably become the world's largest sequoia.

Though relatively little grove land is privately owned in the Sierra Nevada, a small parcel of the Nelder Grove is owned by Cal Tech, a reminder that some rare sequoia resources are still in private hands. That parcel includes a specimen twenty feet in diameter.

Another grove curiosity is an unusual number of tall, lightning-killed sequoia snags. The oldest known non-fossilized sequoia log, dating to about 10,000 years ago, is in a drainage near but outside of the present grove, indicating that the grove was once larger.

MCKINLEY GROVE

Size: Small
Condition: Old growth
Manager: Sierra National Forest
Access: Paved road

McKinley Grove, bisected by the paved McKinley Grove Road, east of Shaver Lake in the Sierra National Forest, is a small old growth "island" grove, surrounded by timberland that has been heavily-managed for timber production for decades. More isolated in distance from the other groves than any but the Placer Grove, it is almost forty air miles from the Nelder Grove on the north, and separated from the Converse Basin Grove on the south by about fifteen air miles and the chasm of Kings Canyon.

McKinley Grove.

The grove has about 150 large sequoias, including about fifty-five over ten feet in diameter (at breast height), spread over about eighty acres of basin and slopes. Though it lacks specimens in the largest size class, a few sequoias approach twenty feet in diameter. Logs include that of the once largest sequoia in the grove, which naturally fell in the 1970s.

McKinley is one of the roadside groves that can be appreciated easily. Most of the grove can be seen from the road, and the grove's limits are a short hike beyond. There is only one short interpretive trail, but cross-country exploration of the small grove is not daunting. Some of the non-sequoia conifers were harvested here in the 1980s—the only episode of grove logging besides that required for road construction. The national champion white fir once grew nearby in the highly productive mixed conifer forest belt. The grove is generally open and scenic despite recent logging impacts. Gigantea Campground is nearby.

GROVES IN THE SOUTHERN KINGS RIVER WATERSHED

CONVERSE BASIN GROVE 31

INDIAN BASIN GROVE 37

CHERRY GAP GROVE 39

BIG STUMP GROVE 40

GRANT GROVE 41

SEQUOIA CREEK GROVE 44

BEARSKIN AND LANDSLIDE GROVES 46

LOCKWOOD GROVE 47

EVANS GROVE 49

KENNEDY GROVE 53

LITTLE BOULDER CREEK GROVE 55

BOULDER CREEK GROVE 55

DEER MEADOW, AGNEW, AND 56
MONARCH GROVES

CONVERSE BASIN GROVE

Size: Very large
Condition: Logged
Manager: Sequoia National Forest
Access: Dirt road

Converse Basin Grove is one of the largest sequoia grove in total area. From a subjective viewpoint, it may have been the most impressive of all the groves in its primeval (about 1890) condition. Regrettably, it was the site of the most destructive early sequoia logging. Probably more mature and old growth sequoias were cut here than in all other groves combined. Though there is no inventory of its lost primeval sequoia forest, it is possible that the Converse Basin at one time contained more mature and old growth sequoias, and more sequoias of exceptionally large size, than any other grove. Despite the destruction that occurred, the grove remains an amazing site, not only as a globally significant historic forest location, but as a collection of scattered old growth specimens and clusters, and home to the most expansive young sequoia stands of post-logging regeneration to be found in any grove.

View over Kings Canyon to Comb Spur from Converse Basin Grove.

The Converse Basin Grove would be considered huge if it filled only the vast bowl encompassed by the Kings Canyon escarpment and the Converse Mountain, Hoist, and west basin ridges, an area about 2.7 air miles wide. However, the grove sprawls well beyond into two western basins (the west basin of Converse Creek and Verplank Creek), into the upper Kings Canyon west of Converse Creek, around the slopes of Converse Mountain, into the sizeable "Cabin Creek Grove," into one major basin west of Hoist Ridge, and to pockets south of Hoist Ridge. Grove elevations range from about 6,700 feet on Hoist Ridge to about 5,400 feet in lower Verplank Creek. The grove covers approximately 3,500 to 3,800 acres of actual sequoia occurrence.

The Boole Tree, the largest sequoia on national forest land, is the most impressive surviving specimen in the grove. It contends with two other living sequoias for distinction as the sixth largest in overall volume. Its ground perimeter (113 feet) and its diameter at sixteen feet above the ground (24.3 feet) reflect this immensity. Perhaps due to the effects of a major 1928 fire, the Boole Tree's upper crown foliage has declined dramatically in size in recent decades.

Widely scattered throughout the grove are many mature sequoias besides the famous old growth Boole Tree. These include the largest surviving old growth group, located along Cabin Creek in Kings Canyon—probably more than twenty-five specimens. This is a fine, preserved "grove within a grove," accessed via a trail offering spectacular Kings Canyon vistas.

The Converse Basin has the most extensive and most impressive young sequoia stands of any logged grove. These young sequoia trees are often of varying ages, and give the appearance of older forests because they have grown so quickly and because they are mixed with multiple sequoias that likely exceed 120 years in age. The grove has the potential to return to an old growth condition within a few centuries, though it still will be a far younger forest than it was about 1890.

Large areas of the Converse Basin Grove cover plateau and basin-like terrain where heavy concentrations of exceptionally large sequoias occur (as in the Giant Forest and Mountain Home Groves). Much of the grove has gentle sloped growing sites with deep soils and ample moisture—ideal sequoia growing conditions. Today, the old growth sequoia stumps hint at the forest that was lost there, just as ancient ruins give rise to images of lost civilizations.

Seasonal grove access is relatively easy on a few dirt roads. Until recently, a wider network of dirt roads allowed greater vehicle access. But, because the forest service has, for the time being, stopped maintaining these roads, many of them have become undriveable due to encroaching brush, fallen trees, and ruts. These routes now serve as unofficial trails. The mostly gentle slopes and largely open character of the forest make cross-country exploration uncomplicated in non-brushy areas. The only maintained trail is the route to the Boole Tree. Converse Basin Grove has no public facilities, but the grove's large size and many small creeks (which have abundant water in early season), provide ample opportunities for secluded, scenic camping.

Former Resources

Before 1890, the grove was filled with high densities of old growth sequoias, and the finest quality of Sierra Nevada mixed conifer forest. There were exceptionally large trees, as indicated by a journalist's commercially-oriented 1895 description, "Here one is surrounded with these giants . . . and as one looks over the Converse Basin, stretching away to walls of the Kings River Canyon, there seems to be no limit to their number. . . Trees scaling from fifty to eighty thousand [board] feet are common, and one group of nine within a space of one hundred feet square averaged sixty thousand [board] feet."

The grove's General Noble Tree (now called the Chicago Stump) was probably the largest sequoia ever cut, according to expert Wendell Flint. It was definitely a "top ten" tree in total volume. The huge, 133-foot-tall Muir Snag, which died before the logging era, could be the remnant of the largest giant sequoia ever. In its fire-damaged condition, without bark and sapwood, it is still larger than the General Sherman Tree at breast height. This may be the "stump" with "4,000 rings" that John Muir imprecisely described finding in his 1875 exploration of the Sierra's sequoia groves. Flint has estimated that it reached about 3,500 years of age, the greatest known sequoia longevity. Several of the logged Converse giants exceeded 3,000 years in age when cut.

Converse Basin Grove had many exceptionally old sequoias. An early twentieth century study of 220 grove stumps identified fifty-three that exceeded two thousand years of age.

Considering that sequoia grove areas are among the most pro-

3024. California Big Trees. Lumber Crew at Booles Tree. Circumference 109 ft.

Hand-tinted early photo of the Boole Tree.

The Boole Tree in 1997.

Though no one seriously asserts that logging has eliminated a sequoia grove, the view that logging has permanently ruined a grove or stripped it of all its special qualities is often taken. However, because a grove was once heavily cut does not mean that it has lost its significance, that it cannot regain an old growth forest character, or that it no longer needs careful stewardship.

Converse Basin Grove provides a good example of the tendency of some to devalue the current sequoia resources of logged groves. Though severely logged during the 1890-1907 period, it retains more than one hundred scattered mature sequoias, including a preserved old growth "grove within a grove" in the Cabin Creek drainage. On the popular visitor route to the Boole Tree trailhead, surviving old growth sequoias are visible only a few hundred yards west of the grove's famous Stump Meadow. Yet, some authors have described the Converse Basin Grove as if no giant sequoias survived the early logging.

Values of Logged Groves

Logged grove areas retain a number of important present and future sequoia values. First, most grove areas that suffered logging were not totally cleared of all their mature trees. For example, heavily-logged Nelder Grove includes over one hundred old growth sequoias, more than occur in many unlogged groves. Other areas that experienced cutting, but still boast many surviving mature and old growth sequoias include parts of Evans Grove, Redwood Mountain Grove (the University of California's Whitaker Forest section), and Mountain Home Grove, as well as Converse Basin Grove.

At the same time, the remaining sequoia stumps, logs, snags, and log fragments in logged areas are fascinating remnants. Many sequoia stumps provide the opportunity to review thousands of years of environmental history, as reflected in tree rings. It is not difficult to find stumps of sequoias that are more than two thousand years old in the Converse Basin Grove, and stumps aged over a thousand years occur in most groves where old growth sequoias were logged.

Further, many logged grove areas contain sequoias that, while not old growth, are significantly older (two hundred years old or more) than the trees that have grown since logging was completed. This is the case because lumbermen often focused on the larger trees only. These neither "old" nor "young" sequoias are often five to seven feet in diameter (at breast height).

Finally, thanks to good growing conditions, usually excellent sequoia regeneration, and rapid young sequoia growth, many of the logged grove areas have recovered a scenic appearance dominated by impressive medium-sized sequoias. Many of these trees are now three to six feet in diameter, and some may grow to become "giants" with diameters of eight feet or more within the next century. Though some logged grove areas have suffered long-term degradation, many grove sites can soon recover a number of old growth forest characteristics. Such places should still be regarded as prime grove areas deserving of protection.

Giant sequoia log, Converse Basin.

ductive sites (in standing timber volume) in Sierra Nevada forests, it is possible that the Converse Basin Grove was the most productive, for its size, in the historic era. In all probability, only California's highest volume coast redwood forests surpassed the Converse Basin in standing timber volume for a comparable area before logging. High volume sites included the famous Stump Meadow (with over one hundred sequoia stumps in the meadow itself) and a smaller "stump meadow" (with forty to fifty stumps) near Hoist Ridge. These old growth forests areas are now meadows because, once the sequoias that used the abundant ground water were logged, the subsurface water table rose too high for most trees to survive.

Converse Basin Mill. Note cable railway running up to Hoist Ridge at left center.

Logging History

Substantial grove logging did not commence until 1893, when the narrow gauge Sequoia Railroad of the Kings River Lumber Company was extended seven miles from its base at the now-vanished sawmill community of Millwood to a point south of Hoist Ridge and the heart of the grove. The Camp 3 logging center was established in that year near the rail terminus, in upper Goodmill Creek (at the site of the small Cherry Gap Grove). A cable railway hoist was constructed from the rail terminus up to the south edge of the grove on what became known as Hoist Ridge, and the first extensive sequoia logging in the grove commenced. Initially, steam donkeys hauled logs from the grove to the top of the incline, later to

Giant sequoia survivors west of Stump Meadow.

be replaced by a fixed power hoist housed in a sizeable building at a saddle on the ridge.

Grove logging continued through the 1896 season, but results were erratic and unprofitable. Logs were transported by the Sequoia Railroad to the Millwood Mill, and not milled in the grove vicinity. Lumber was floated from Millwood to Sanger in the Central Valley by way of a fifty-four-mile flume through the Kings Canyon wilderness. This amazing flume had been built in 1889-90 to service the initial Kings River Lumber Company operations.

In an effort to make its operations profitable, the renamed Sanger Company intensified logging in the Converse Basin. During the winter of 1896–97, the Converse Mill was constructed in the lower basin, astride Converse Creek, and the railway incline was extended to it from Hoist Ridge. The mill started operating in 1897. By the time it burned down in November 1905, almost all of the old growth sequoias in the grove had been destroyed.

Between 1897 and 1905, believed to be the grove's most intensive sequoia logging period, as many as six to seven hundred men worked in logging operations throughout the basin. Numerous "chutes" of parallel logs and skidways fed two main chutes to the Converse Mill. By 1901 or 1902 logs were hoisted and chuted to the mill from Indian Basin Grove to the east. Because the mill had a "redwood splitter," called the largest band saw in the world at the time, it could handle logs of any size, making even the largest sequoias candidates for cutting. Many sequoias over twenty feet in diameter were milled. From the Converse Mill, finished lumber was lifted on a railroad hoist about three miles up Hoist Ridge, lowered to the railroad terminus, and transported to Millwood by rail.

In December 1905, after the first Converse Mill burned, a group headed by Thomas Hume acquired the Sanger Company assets. By July 1906, the new Sanger ownership had built a second Converse Mill on the same site. "Mop-up" logging in the basin continued in 1906 and 1907, along with new logging in a basin on the west side of Hoist Ridge. By 1908, major logging in Converse Basin ceased.

The movable logging equipment, including the single railroad loco-motive, was relocated to support the new mill of the Hume-Bennett Lumber Company at Hume Lake. The Converse Mill was then deliberately burned. The town of Millwood was soon abandoned; nothing now remains of it.

The recorded harvest in the Converse Basin during the nine years of intense cutting (from 1897 to 1905) totaled 191 million board feet (an average of 21.2 million board feet per year). The greatest cut was in 1903 - about 26.2 million board feet. Surprisingly, historic photos indicate that the logging was selective, except for clearcut areas like the Converse Mill site. In particular, the loggers appeared to ignore small saw timber and some mature white fir. Post-logging fires, however, duplicated the effect of clearcutting over much of the grove.

The lost world of Converse Basin on the rim of Kings Canyon.

Only minor logging of standing timber occurred between 1907 (when the Sanger Company moved out) and the major McGee Fire in the grove in 1955. There was also substantial unrecorded harvest of the abundant down sequoia wood that remained after the early logging.

Most fire- and insect-damaged trees in the grove were harvested after the 1955 McGee Fire, primarily along Hoist Ridge and in the southwestern part of the grove. Starting in the late 1970s, the forest service resumed cutting in the grove, the first known major harvest of undamaged green sequoias in the actual Converse Basin since 1907. This culminated in the mid-1980s with very heavy logging, including clearcuts of non-sequoia conifers and cutting of young sequoias, in several areas of the grove. These recent cuts are still conspicuous, particularly a huge clearcut in the heart of the basin, south of the Converse Mill site.

INDIAN BASIN GROVE

Size: Mid-size
Condition: Logged
Manager: Sequoia National Forest
Access: Paved road

Indian Basin Grove, in Sequoia National Forest, was an extremely fine, mid-sized grove (about 160 acres) with dense large sequoias before it was totally logged of old growth by the Sanger Lumber Company between 1901 and 1908. At least 150, and possibly as many as 200 mature sequoias were cut. The timber was hauled west and about 700 feet up the Rob Roy Hoist cable railway to the crest of Converse Mountain Ridge (between the Converse and Indian Basin Groves), then transported down log chutes to the Converse Mill.

Now bisected by Highway 180, the grove is at a somewhat lower elevation (5,900 to 6,000 feet) than most southern groves, and has an atypical southern exposure. Its non-sequoia conifers are characteristic of those found in the lower elevations of the mixed conifer forest zone, with relatively more pines and incense cedar. Normally, southern Sierra groves at higher elevations with northern exposures are associated with white fir or white fir/sugar pine forests.

North of the highway, the grove includes some relatively young, but tall and mature-looking sequoias with diameters of six feet or more. These trees are impressively large for being less than a century old. Young sequoias seem to have been spared in the mid-twentieth century selective logging in the grove, and are thriving. Current U.S. Forest Service policy prohibits commercial logging there.

The basin-like terrain of the grove was ideal for the growth of very large and ancient specimens. Though it covered a relatively small area, the primeval grove almost certainly had sections comparable to the most impressive sequoia stands anywhere, as one can readily imagine on a cross-country hike through the stumpland north of the highway. Due to the gentle and meadowy terrain and dense stump concentrations, the grove is one of the easiest in which to casually survey a range of impressively sized sequoia stumps. Pioneer dendrochronologist Ellsworth Huntington found three stumps of trees over two thousand years old, and abundant stumps of trees over a thousand years. Here, as in the Converse Basin Grove, the stumps are larger, on average, than those in many other logged grove areas (such as in Evans Grove) to the east.

The meadowy sections north of the highway are a creation of the higher water table which followed the early logging. Abundant large stumps in the meadow suggest that the open, sunny meadow was once a cathedral forest penetrated only by shafts of sunlight. If protected, the vigorous second growth in this moist site can restore such majestic conditions in centuries to come.

Large Princess Campground is in the grove; giant stumps are sprinkled among the campsites, along with young and mid-aged sequoias and mixed conifers. Adjacent Indian Meadow is one of the largest and most beautiful meadows in the area, with inspiring views of the Monarch Divide to the northeast. Indian Creek was populated by beaver as late as the 1970s.

Sequoia stumps in meadow at Indian Basin Grove.

CHERRY GAP GROVE

Size: Small
Condition: Logged, with only young sequoias
Manager: Sequoia National Forest
Access: Dirt road

A small grove of about thirty-five acres in Sequoia National Forest, Cherry Gap was logged of all its old growth sequoias (approximately twenty-five trees) in the early 1890s by the Kings River Lumber Company, which later extended its cutting into the Converse Basin Grove. The grove is in the basin of the headwaters of Goodmill Creek, in the large basin overlooked by the McGee viewpoint on Highway 180 on the east and bordered by the south slopes of Hoist Ridge on the north. It is bisected by an old rail bed (see below), which currently is a usable, low standard, seasonal dirt road. Access is best from the south.

Cherry Gap Grove.

The grove area was a busy transfer point from 1893-1908, connecting the cable railway hoist from the Converse Basin Grove to the north with the Sequoia Railroad line to Millwood. First raw logs, and later (after the Converse Mill was built) milled boards were switched from hoist car to rail car in Cherry Gap Grove. From Millwood the timber was floated in a fifty-four mile flume to the Central Valley. Cherry Gap was also the site of the small Upper Abbott Mill, which primarily milled pine and fir.

Artifacts remaining from the early logging era and much of the forest that had regenerated after the original logging activity were destroyed by the intense 1955 McGee Fire that devastated a total of eighteen thousand acres, including Hoist Ridge and most of the basin surrounding the grove. The fire was followed by intensive salvage logging. The Cherry Gap Grove is now a relatively nondescript young forest, contrasting with the wall of tall, green timber to the south beyond the burned area, near the boundary of Kings Canyon National Park. It is difficult to imagine the grove as an old growth sequoia forest or as a busy station during the heyday of logging activity.

The grove is sprinkled with small, young, healthy, "spire top" sequoias. Indistinct charred features observed from a distance prove on close examination to be the remnants of sequoias once over ten feet in diameter. While most of the young growth is less than forty years old, one pocket on the north edge of the grove has advanced young sequoias from four to six feet in diameter (at breast height) that survived the 1955 fire. In general, however, the sequoias in this grove are much younger than the regenerated sequoias in several other groves cut in the early logging era.

Cherry Gap Grove is quiet, well-watered, and lushly vegetated with smaller trees and shrub species, which hide most of the sequoia stumps. A stump-hunter will have far better luck in early spring before the dogwood, oaks, and willows of this largely deciduous young forest blanket them with foliage. Under current forest service protection policy, the grove should slowly recover its original character as a conifer-dominated, vigorous little sequoia grove.

It's possible to imagine the old railroad experience by driving the narrow, winding rail route from the Millwood site south and west of the grove. The gentle-graded course, with many deep rail cuts, differs from the usual forest service dirt roads. Of course, road alterations adjusted for the now-missing twenty-three trestles that were part of the seven-mile Sequoia Railroad line between Millwood and Cherry Gap Grove.

Two tiny, isolated sites with a few old growth sequoia stumps and pockets of young sequoias are found just south of the rail route in tributary draws of Abbott Creek, well west of Cherry Gap Grove. They have been called the "Abbott Creek Grove." But these trees are more reasonably considered to be occasional "outliers"—scattered sequoias which occur near but outside of recognized "groves."

BIG STUMP GROVE

Size: Mid-size
Condition: Logged, with a few old growth sequoias
Manager: Kings Canyon National Park and Sequoia National Forest
Access: Paved road

Big Stump Grove is the first a visitor encounters upon entering the Sierra Nevada on Highway 180. A mid-sized grove covering several hundred acres, it extends from almost unvisited lower elevations in Sequoia National Forest into the well-touristed Kings Canyon National Park. The Forest Service section of the grove is accessed by a seasonal dirt road that leaves Highway 180 just west of the park entrance. The park section is bisected by the highway, and it has a developed picnic area.

The grove was logged of almost all of its old growth between about 1883 and 1891 by loggers for the Comstock Mill, located in what is now the national park section of the grove. Curiously, tree ring studies show that a surprising number of the logged giants were only in the five hundred to six hundred year age range. Tree ring analysts determined that much of the primeval Big Stump Grove before logging was made up of sequoias that regenerated following an extremely destructive fourteenth-century fire.

This discovery illustrates that a range of sequoia age classes can exist within "mature" or "old growth" groves. Mature sequoia populations can be characterized by relatively younger mature trees (e.g., the Big Stump Grove before it was logged) or older trees (e.g., the Calaveras and Grant Groves) as a result of natural ecosystem dynamics. Big Stump Grove stumps aged at over two thousand years demonstrate that exceptional sequoia specimens can endure even the most destructive prehistoric fires.

A sprinkling of old growth sequoias survives (at least thirteen over ten feet in diameter at breast height, with the largest diameter twenty feet), and there are dense stands of young sequoias. These "young" trees are among the oldest post-logging sequoias in any grove, many of them over a century in age and four to six feet in diameter (at breast height).

The charred Burnt Monarch snag (also known as Old Adam), which died before the historic era, may be the remnant of the largest

A survivor at Big Stump Grove.

Felling the Mark Twain Tree in 1891.   *A section of the Mark Twain log.*

sequoia ever. If its bark and sapwood were to be restored, the tree would be twenty-nine feet in diameter (at breast height), greater than any other known sequoia. It is one of the most impressive sequoia relics.

The grove is named for the stump of the huge Mark Twain Tree. The cutting of the tree in 1891 is documented in some of the most dramatic photographs taken of early sequoia logging. Sections of the Mark Twain Tree are still on display in the New York City Museum of Natural History.

The national park section has an interpretive trail which weaves among the enduring old growth stumps and young sequoias, by the site of the Comstock Mill, and by a feature that shouldn't be missed, the astonishing Burnt Monarch snag.

GRANT GROVE

Size: Small
Condition: Mixed
Manager: Kings Canyon National Park and Sequoia National Forest
Access: Paved road

The Kings Canyon National Park section of Grant Grove (originally named the "General Grant Grove") is peerless in having so many exceptionally large sequoias grouped in so small an area. Within just ninety acres of old growth (accessible by a short spur road off of Highway 180), the National Park Service has counted fifty specimens at least fifteen feet in diameter (at breast height), including ten trees at least twenty feet in diameter. A far higher percentage of the

Right: The General Grant Tree.

Below: Early photo of the General Grant Tree, by C.C. Curtis.

grove's mature sequoias reach sizes of ten, fifteen, and twenty feet in diameter than in any other grove. The explanation for this concentration of huge sequoias remains a mystery, but visitors will find the trees a feast for the eyes and spirit.

The grove's most famous feature is the General Grant Tree, honored each year as "the nation's Christmas tree." The Grant Tree is an utterly awe-inspiring specimen, recognized as the third largest sequoia, exceeded only by the General Sherman and Washington Trees of Giant Forest. It has the largest known diameter (28.9 feet at breast height) of any living sequoia, and a height of about 267 feet. The park service has cleared a medium-distance vista of the tree, offering visitors one of the best opportunities they will find anywhere to photograph a large sequoia from top to bottom.

The General Grant Tree.

The grove was one of the foremost sequoia attractions for nineteenth-century tourists. Early sightseers were so aggressive that John Muir described the General Grant Tree in 1873 as "barbarously destroyed by visitors hacking off chips and engraving their names in all styles." No one today would suspect these past abuses given the Grant's present restored natural appearance. General Grant National Park, encompassing a small area around the grove, was created in 1890 to protect it.

Early 1890s loggers had their will in the western section of the grove, which is now in Sequoia National Forest. The west grove flanks descending Big Tree Creek. This deserted grove section is accessible by trail from the park or from a forest service dirt road on the west. At least twenty large sequoias were cut there, leaving the high stumps characteristic of the earliest sequoia logging period. The forest around the stumps, including abundant, tall stands of young sequoias, has been largely undisturbed since the logging a century ago, and, except for the remarkable stumps, it has recovered a scenic forest character. The logged giants won't be replaced for centuries, but this area shows how attractive a second-growth mixed conifer forest can become in a century.

The Grant Tree section of the grove is a model of a meticulously managed "showcase" old growth sequoia display. Highly managed for intensive tourism for nearly a century, the Grant Tree area has had its vegetation manipulated by manual removal and by controlled burning to promote an open forest character, full of sequoia vistas. Overall, the section is not a representative grove landscape.

As a small living sequoia "museum" exhibit, however, the Grant Grove is the perfect place to see glorious mammoth trees in an extremely scenic setting. It is highly recommended! To avoid midsummer crowds, visit early or late in the day, or explore the excellent trail network beyond the Grant Tree area.

The main interpretive trail passes several enormous sequoias besides the General Grant Tree. These include the General Lee Tree, another of the world's fifteen largest trees, the Oregon Tree, the unsigned Lincoln Tree, and the California Tree. The California Tree lost twenty-five feet of its top to lightning in 1967; tree-climbing park service firefighters extinguished its treetop fire.

The trail also accesses the Centennial Stump, remnant of another of the Sierra largest sequoias. It was illegally cut in 1875, to the

Fog moving through the Muir Grove.

chagrin of John Muir, who happened upon the tragedy and calculated that the tree was about 2,250 years old. Away from the main trail, the Dead Giant is a standing snag (nearly twenty feet in diameter at breast height) that was killed by girdling axe-cuts. Unfortunately, even grove areas that received early national park protection did not always escape unscathed by loggers.

The North Grove trail loop has abundant sequoias, though none are famous or extraordinarily large. There the park service has implemented controlled burning in recent years, intended to reduce the unnatural fire hazard created by over-dense understory vegetation.

The Grant Grove is closest to the tiny pockets of outlying sequoias in southern draws of the Abbott Creek drainage, discussed earlier, which have been called the "Abbott Creek Grove," though the areas are separated by a divide.

SEQUOIA CREEK GROVE

Size: Tiny
Condition: Mixed
Manager: Kings Canyon National Park and private owners
Access: Trail

Just south of Grant Grove, in Kings Canyon National Park, is the very small Sequoia Creek Grove. About twenty-five mature sequoias are concentrated in about ten pristine acres along the creek with its

Sequoias live longer than all other tree species except the bristlecone pines *(Pinus longaeva)* of the Great Basin mountain ranges and the Alerce tree of Chile and Argentina. The sequoia was believed to be the longest-lived organism until 1958, when bristlecones aged over 4,000 years were discovered. The oldest bristlecone, growing on Nevada's Wheeler Peak, was estimated to be about 4,900 years of age when it was carelessly cut. The oldest known sequoia, the dead Muir Snag in Converse Basin Grove, is estimated to have lived about 3,500 years. It is possible that older sequoia specimens are still living.

It is difficult to determine the age of a sequoia without cutting into its center and potentially harming it. Such practice is gen-erally prohibited. The ages of many famous trees have not been verified. However, when a sufficiently large portion of a tree's annual rings is exposed in fire scars, age data can be obtained by non-destructive, short increment borings. This method allows fairly reliable age estimations within a range of several centuries. Counts of the exposed rings on several sequoia stumps have placed specimen ages at over 3,000 years.

Trees over 1,500 and even 2,000 years old are common in some groves. Sequoias over 1,000 years of age are abundant. Depending on their terrain and past vulnerability to intense fires, some groves have a higher percentage of ancient specimens than others.

picturesque Ella Falls. Despite its small size, this unlogged grove has about fifteen specimens at least ten feet in diameter (at breast height), including one that is twenty-one feet, as well as old growth mixed conifers and younger sequoias. Outlying young sequoias also extend down along Sequoia Creek to the shores of Sequoia Lake onto once-logged private land west of the park. Big Stump Grove is just south of the grove.

The section of Kings Canyon National Park including Grant and Sequoia Creek Groves is, like several other grove areas, part of a relatively small island of old growth habitat, surrounded by an area where logging has largely eliminated old growth.

BEARSKIN AND LANDSLIDE GROVES

Size: Small
Condition: Old growth
Manager: Sequoia National Forest
Access: Bearskin Grove—dirt road; Landslide Grove—trail (closed dirt road)

Bearskin and Landslide Groves are two small Sequoia National Forest groups in the upper Tenmile Creek watershed, south of Hume Lake. They were beyond the reach of early loggers, and all of their old growth sequoias survive. Their non-sequoia conifers were partially logged, commencing decades ago. Current forest service policy prohibits further commercial logging. The groves are small islands of old growth habitat in a once prime Sierra watershed that has been stripped of virtually all of its old growth trees in logging operations since the Hume Lake Mill opened in 1909.

Bearskin Grove has two close units (on opposite sides of a small hill), totalling about sixty acres. There are no grove trails. The larger east unit has easy dirt road access and retains some significant old growth mixed conifer stands. The grove has about eighty-five sequoias over six feet in diameter (at breast height), including one tree in each unit that approaches twenty feet in diameter, and numerous young sequoias. A vigorous hiker can fully explore Bearskin, with its density of sequoias within a small area, in a day or less.

Bearskin was the first grove impacted when Sequoia National Forest grove management practices shifted in the 1980s from unofficial prohibition against significant cutting to widespread clearcut logging of non-sequoia conifers. Bearskin had been periodically selectively logged for non-sequoia timber, and large isolated stumps and traces of long-abandoned temporary logging skidways can be found within it. Bearskin was an even more impressive grove in fairly recent times.

Both Bearskin Grove units are marred by eight to nine acre cuts where nearly all of the non-sequoia conifers were cut in the early 1980s. The east unit is striking visually with more than fifteen surviving giants standing on a bare clearcut slope above the access road. The cut contrasts disturbingly with the fine old growth sequoia-sugar pine forest just across the road. Two fire-damaged sequoias have naturally fallen in the east unit since 1990.

Bearskin giant.

Unlike some grove sites logged before 1920, the east Bearskin clearcut did not regenerate well. After post-logging burning, the cut became dominated by whitethorn brush, which can retard forest regeneration for decades. This rapidly growing, thick brush (up to five feet high) overshaded sun-starved sequoia and pine seedlings. The only two large pines spared by the loggers died. The sequoia saplings now overtopping the brush (most of which were manually planted by the forest service and protected from brush by hand clearing for many years afterwards) are thriving, and the site will probably recover its coniferous forest character eventually.

On the ridge between the two Bearskin Grove units is a young, unnatural plantation consisting of Jeffrey pines only. Such small, singles-species tree plantations were typical, post-logging treatments for decades prior to the 1980s; explorers will encounter these plantations in many groves. In contrast, current Sequoia National Forest policy prescribes reforestation of logged sites with a natural diversity of conifer types.

Landslide Grove, in the headwaters area of Landslide Creek a few miles east of Bearskin Grove, has sequoias densely packed in two units that total over one hundred acres. It is primarily old growth forest, though heavy logging came right to the grove's edges. Roads to the grove have been closed, so it is accessible by hiking; the grove's extremely steep terrain and its absence of trails make exploration quite difficult. There are probably fifty to one hundred mature sequoias, none of which is exceptionally large. A proposal to add Landslide, Bearskin, and other groves east of Hume Lake to Sequoia National Park passed the U.S. Senate in 1919, but never became law.

LOCKWOOD GROVE

Size: Small
Condition: Mixed
Manager: Sequoia National Forest.
Access: Primitive dirt road

Lockwood is a small, two-unit grove located on a slope in Sequoia National Forest. Its old growth section is in the headwaters of Lockwood Creek, spectacularly set against the northern backdrop of vast Kings Canyon. Across its chasm, Spanish Mountain (10,051 feet) stands more than 7,500 feet above the Kings River. The views of the gorge seen beyond the red trunks of the Lockwood Grove giants emphasize the ironic fact that some of the world's largest trees grow on the rim of North America's deepest canyon.

There are about eighty to ninety mature sequoias in the main Lockwood Creek unit, including exceptionally tall specimens. The northern exposure and white fir and sugar pine forest components of much of the grove are typical of southern Sierra groves. When viewed from the east in the morning sun, the dense red trunks descending the slopes along the creek appear like a wall of giants.

Most of the grove's sequoias are not remarkably large, a fact probably attributable to the greater frequency of severe fires in the

Lockwood Grove.

Fire scar.

grove's canyon setting over the centuries. The most recent intense fire in 1931 killed several giants, which were harvested for timber. At the lower edge of the grove, the fire's effects are still evident from three charred sequoia snags, a dense creekside stand of more than a hundred very young sequoias that probably regenerated soon after the fire, and a slope covered with hardwoods rather than conifers.

The Forest Service seasonal dirt access road, east of Hume Lake, partially follows the railbed of the Hume-Bennett Lumber Co. logging railroad, which operated through the grove between 1911 and 1918. (The railroad logging is further described in the Evans Grove section.) Lockwood Grove was the nearest to the Hume Lake Mill, and the loggers quickly cut all of the sequoias (except for one roadside survivor) in the grove's small western unit (once named the "Camp 4 Grove" after the adjacent logging camp). That unit is on extremely steep slopes in the headwaters of Barton Flat Creek, below the present road. A cable railway hoist was used to lift the timber to the main railroad line.

The single surviving giant and a few spire-top young sequoias in the west Lockwood unit hardly hint that this area now dominated by young pines and oaks was once a small grove with probably twenty old growth trees. Its stumps hidden from all but the most curious bushwhackers, the unit is one that was logged into near invisibility.

In a puzzling quirk, early private timber claimholders, who had acquired most of the grove land in the present Hume Ranger

District, failed to acquire title to the Lockwood Creek grove unit. It remained in forest service hands. The lumber company obtained only a railroad right-of-way, which allowed them to conduct their logging in Evans Grove to the east. Ironically, a fallen empire of dead Evans Grove giants passed through Lockwood Grove on the way to the Hume Mill, but the beautiful Lockwood Creek sequoias were spared.

The Lockwood Creek section was preserved as a small island of old growth until the non-sequoia forest east of the creek and below the rail bed was nearly clearcut of non-sequoia conifers in the mid-1980s. A narrow part of the grove west of Lockwood Creek retains the full complement of mature sequoia forest conifers. It is a meager relic of the once vast stands of old growth that perched above the Kings Canyon escarpment, from Converse Basin on the west to Evans Grove on the east.

The perceptive observer might wonder why Lockwood Grove lacks the density of fallen logs common in other unlogged sequoia groves (particularly those in national parks). Being accessible by road, this forest service grove (and others) saw its fallen sequoias routinely harvested for timber for several decades. In some groves, standing sequoia snags were also taken down, as only living old growth sequoias were protected. In 1990 the forest service adopted a policy of preserving fallen sequoia logs.

The trail-less grove is relatively easy to explore cross-country, despite some steep terrain.

EVANS GROVE

Size: Large
Condition: Mixed
Manager: Sequoia National Forest
Access: Primitive dirt road

Evans Grove in Sequoia National Forest is one of the largest, with dramatic backdrop views of Kings Canyon, Monarch Divide peaks, and the distant Sierra Crest. Much of the western section of the grove was logged before 1920, and abundant stumps and vestiges of the early railroad construction give the grove unusual historic interest. Major unlogged sections of the grove are dense with spectacular old growth sequoias.

Not readily accessible, the Evans Grove can be reached by seasonal dirt road, and explored on foot using several old, revegetating dirt roads, or cross-country. A dirt road winds about three miles through the grove. Currently, lack of maintenance makes it inaccessible to vehicles. It and the trail that continues east through the roadless eastern old growth section of the grove roughly follow the rail bed route of the Hume-Bennett logging railroad that operated between the grove and the Hume Lake Mill between 1914 and 1918. The half-mile eastern extension of the rail bed beyond the end of the present road was cleared, but logging operations ceased before rail was laid. It is now a wide trail. The nearly level road and trail pro-

Evans Grove view over Redwood Creek to Kings Canyon.

Evans Grove view north to Windy Cliffs and Tehipite Dome.

vide excellent access, bisecting the grove from east to west beneath the steepest upper drainage slopes and above sequoia-filled basins.

Because it is not highly visited, the grove gives the visitor a feeling of remoteness and wilderness, despite its dirt roads and historical impacts. In fact, the grove section below 6,400 feet elevation is included in the Monarch Wilderness area. More of the grove is in de facto wilderness condition.

The grove is generally bounded by distinct geographic features. Its west and south edges are close to ridges. An 8,152-foot peak crowns the south ridge above the central grove, which reaches the grove's upper elevation limit of about 7,400 feet. The east grove edge is demarcated partially by the sharp fall-off of Boulder Creek Canyon and partially by a ridge. On the north, the grove reaches its limits between about 4,800 and 6,000 feet elevation in Kings Canyon. Evans Grove grandly sweeps over more than 2,000 feet of elevation range.

Almost all of the grove is contained in the well-defined main drainages of Redwood Creek, Windy Gulch, and Evans Creek (from west to east). Though all of these watersheds have ample sequoias, grove sections differ markedly in their forest make-up. Redwood Creek, Windy Gulch, and the western section of Evans Creek are dominated by second growth forest (with scattered surviving old growth sequoias), reflecting intensive sequoia logging from 1914 to 1918, and some subsequent logging. In dramatic, abrupt contrast, the grove in the east section of the Evans Creek watershed is characterized by a spectacular, unlogged area with abundant old growth sequoia, extending from ridge top to canyon depths. This unlogged section is equivalent in size to a medium-sized old growth grove.

The grove probably has more than five hundred surviving mature and old growth sequoias. These are concentrated in the unlogged eastern Evans Creek section, but there are also numerous surviving old growth clusters on the slopes above the rail bed in the Windy Gulch drainage, in lower Windy Gulch and an east tributary canyon, and in the once-named "Horseshoe Bend Grove" section of the upper Redwood Creek watershed. Several scattered giants, amid abundant post-logging sequoia growth, survive in areas heavily logged by 1918. Three such trees are beside the road at the head of Redwood Creek basin, and another, larger, isolated survivor with a huge fire scar cavity is just below the road in Windy Gulch basin.

Evans Grove never had as many exceptionally large sequoias (proportionally) as large groves set in gentler terrain (like Giant Forest, Converse Basin, and Mountain Home Groves). Though the basins of Redwood Creek and Windy Gulch had very dense sequoia stands, as remaining stumps show, most of the trees were relatively small for mature sequoias (a very few specimens are about twenty feet in diameter at breast height). Evans Grove's canyon locale has subjected it to more frequent intense fires through the millennia than groves with gentler terrain, and far fewer specimens have lived to be fifteen hundred years old or more.

In trail-less lower Windy Gulch, at about 6,000 feet, one of the grove's most dramatic, isolated, and grizzled old snag-top survivors endures across Kings Canyon from precipitous Windy Cliffs.

Since their discovery, sequoias have inspired rhapsodic human reactions. John Muir called the sequoia "nature's masterpiece," "the greatest of living things," a "king tree," and "the very god of the woods." Upon visiting the sequoias, early writers quickly exhausted their supply of superlatives. Primal awe rather than understanding is still likely to dominate the appreciative passion of even the most informed student of sequoias.

There is something otherworldly about sequoia trees. Early twentieth century traveler Joseph Smeaton Chase romanticized, "In them we have what seems to be the last survival of the Heroic Age of the earth, that misty dawn of time when all things, perhaps man included, reached the gigantic in stature and age. They are an anachronism, an unaccountable oversight, a kind of arboreal Rip Van Winkle. . ." Muir reflected that sequoia groves are "not like places, they are like haunts."

Sequoias have inspired fresh and enduring wonder and awe in all types of visitors, from turn-of-the-century poets to objective modern scientists and recreational visitors. As is the Grand Canyon, the sequoias are a marvel that words and photographs represent, but can't well communicate. To be in their majestic presence is always stunning, no matter how much one expects to be familiar with them.

Evans Grove snag-topped survivor above Kings Canyon.

Logging History

The Hume-Bennett Lumber Co. (renamed the Sanger Lumber Co. in 1917) intensively logged the grove between 1914 and 1918 with the help of a remarkable logging railroad extending from its Hume Lake Mill through Lockwood Grove and into the interior of the grove as far as "Camp 7" on the Windy Gulch/Evans Creek divide. The grove was then private timberland. Lumber was transported from the Hume Mill through Kings Canyon to Sanger in the Central Valley by the phenomenal flume, which originally had been built to serve the Millwood mills to the west. When Converse Basin Grove logging operations ended in 1907, the flume from Millwood to the canyon was abandoned, and a new connection was built from Hume Lake, down Tenmile Creek, to the existing Kings Canyon flume section. The extended flume totaled fifty-nine miles in length from Hume Lake to Sanger.

Only the Converse Basin Grove lost more mature sequoias to loggers in such a short period of time than did the Evans Grove. The little-heralded and unprotested cutting in the Evans Grove was one of the most noteworthy of all short-term historical assaults on Earth's forest wonders.

In order to transport logs from the Windy Gulch basin, a very short distance west from Camp 7 as the crow flies but at lower elevation, a spur rail line was circuitously extended north from the camp along the east side of the Windy Gulch/Evans Creek divide, then west and around the ridge when its elevation lowered, and back south into the basin. Grove timber was moved to the railroad by parallel log chutes and cable railway hoists powered by steam "donkey" engines. Because the mill couldn't cut logs over 9 feet in diameter, larger logs were split in the grove by blasting before railroad loading.

Though the massive logging ended when the Hume Lake Mill burned in November 1917, a smaller mill was quickly built on the same site, and a final year of major grove logging occurred in 1918. With the onset of World War I and economic recession, the company ceased cutting operations, except for one last season in 1923, which apparently did not affect Evans Grove. Fire damage to the flume in the late 1920s was never repaired, and the threat of resumed Evans Grove logging faded. The forest service finally acquired the grove in 1935.

In the early 1950s, much of the remaining downed and abandoned sequoia wood from early logging operations was harvested. Then in the mid-1970s the grove was substantially impacted by forest service logging, when it managed the first known major harvest of live trees in the grove since 1918. Grove logging was selective, probably for non-sequoia conifers only; mature sequoias and logging artifacts were protected. Several new roads were built. The cutting did not impact any previously unlogged area in the grove. Areas of non-sequoia forest above and adjacent to the upper grove were logged for the first time, however. Current forest service policy protects the grove from further logging.

The grove is full of variety and surprising hidden finds, unnoticed until one stumbles upon them. These could be a giant twenty feet in diameter, huge stumps, stone landings from long-gone railroad trestles, one of the grove's many black bears, or even, as I experienced, an annoyed rattlesnake at an elevation of 6,600 feet.

KENNEDY GROVE

Size: Mid-size
Condition: Old growth
Manager: Sequoia National Forest
Access: Trail (closed dirt road)

Unheralded Kennedy Grove is a very fine, wilderness grove of about 350 to 400 acres in the Boulder Creek watershed of Sequoia National Forest. Almost miraculously it retained its primeval old growth forest character despite the lack of any official protective designation until the 1990s. The grove lacks any trails; it is for the adventurous only.

Early in this century, lumbermen had mapped an ambitious extension of the Evans Grove logging railroad. After the planned destruction of the Evans Grove old growth, the railroad operations would have turned south into the Boulder Creek watershed and stripped the wonders of Kennedy Grove in the 1920s. But the Hume-Bennett/Sanger enterprise ended rail construction in 1917, and the entire logging fury east of Hume Lake came to a stop shortly thereafter. In the 1980s, logging on forest service land reached the Kennedy Grove's south edge, but the grove itself was spared. Forest service policy now protects it from adverse logging impacts. An added measure of protection has been provided by the grove's inclusion in a "Spotted Owl Habitat Area."

The grove is next to a larger block of wild land in Boulder Creek canyon, which extends to the legislated Monarch Wilderness. Above the Kennedy Grove on the ridgetop to the north are the uppermost giants of east Evans Grove. Hikers on that ridge can enjoy a striking southern overview of Kennedy Grove, with Little Boulder Creek Grove beyond in the distance.

The grove has one major unit of complex shape with areas of both dense and scattered sequoias. There are a total of several hundred sequoias. To the north is a small unit along lower Kennedy Meadow Creek with only a few large sequoias.

Most of the mature giants are relatively small (under ten feet in diameter at breast height), but they grow in remarkably high densities in several minor drainages. The grove has one singularly large sequoia, the Ishi Giant, identified by the author in 1993. It has been measured to be the ninth largest known living sequoia.

As is the case with other groves situated in canyons, intense fires have burned this grove more frequently over the centuries, sweeping upslope from the dry, brushy slopes of lower Kings and Boulder Creek Canyons. Unnaturally large buildups of young white fir and woody debris in the grove understory caused by twentieth-century fire suppression have contributed to a very high current fire hazard in Kennedy Grove.

Kennedy Grove extends down to about 5,400 feet, a low elevation

Kennedy Grove overview looking north.

for a southern Sierra grove. The mixed conifer forest includes relatively more pines and less large white fir than the sugar pine-white fir forest associated with the higher elevation or cooler northern exposure sites where most southern Sierra groves are located.

As at comparable southern Sierra elevations, the effects of the drought of the late 1980s took a heavy toll at the Kennedy Grove; insect attacks killed many drought-stressed trees, including several ancient sugar pines five to seven feet in diameter. Most of these large snags will remain standing for decades. They will provide excellent nesting habitat for cavity-dwelling birds. The grove still has impressively huge sugar and ponderosa pines, once characteristic of the primeval forest in the vicinity, but now absent in adjacent forest land managed for commercial timber production.

A two-mile hike on a no-longer-maintained dirt road provides access to the grove's south edge. Those prepared for cross-country going will find enjoyable hidden valleys of gentle terrain, along with difficult, steep, overgrown sections that discourage exploration. One remote spot has a jumble of about seven sequoia logs that probably fell in domino fashion in a past windstorm or other catastrophe. Look also for a top-heavy giant, twenty feet in diameter, that remains standing though its base is nearly half burned away. Don't be surprised to come across black bear, which are common here and in other unlogged sections of Kings Canyon area forests.

LITTLE BOULDER CREEK GROVE

Size: Small
Condition: Old growth
Manager: Sequoia National Forest
Access: Trail (closed dirt road)

Southeast of Kennedy Grove, Little Boulder Creek Grove sits in a tributary drainage of the Boulder Creek watershed of Sequoia National Forest. Though part of the grove was heavily logged for pine and fir by the Forest Service in the 1980s, the grove's sequoias were never cut. Over one hundred large specimens survive. Most of the mature sequoias here are relatively small, compared with the exceptionally large giants of a grove such as Giant Forest. Little Boulder Creek Grove, however, is not without impressive individual specimens reminiscent of those in famous groves. One of the largest is near the unlogged southeast end (top) of the grove, and a second stands beside an abandoned 1980s logging road in the heavily-cut heart of the grove.

Little Boulder Creek Grove with 1980s clearcuts in background.

The grove is accessible by dirt road from the south. Hiking within the grove, cross-country or on closed logging roads, is relatively easy. There are few visitors. The minor drainage descending from the southeast corner of the grove is still pristine, with mature pines, naturally fallen sequoia logs, and many old growth giants. This tiny drainage is another example of a precious island of old growth, mixed conifer forest in a landscape that has been heavily managed for timber production.

Extensive clearcutting of non-sequoia conifers in the 1980s scarred the terrain south and southwest of the grove. In the huge cut by the access road junction southeast of the grove, a single mature sequoia was left. It indicates the height of the mixed conifer forest before logging. This prominent sequoia is an example of an isolated, mature tree occurring near, but outside of, recognized "grove" concentrations, as happens occasionally. Those who continue east towards Boulder Creek past the grove access road junction can spot another isolated mature sequoia on a slope just north of the road.

BOULDER CREEK GROVE

Size: Small
Condition: Old growth
Manager: Sequoia National Forest
Access: Dirt road

The dirt road to Boulder Creek passes through the lower edge of small Boulder Creek Grove, which straddles an unnamed, minor drainage. The grove can be fully explored in a short bushwhack. Though very small, it is a fine refuge for about thirty-five mature sequoias, several sequoia logs, unlogged old growth mixed conifers, and numerous young sequoias —a rare natural preserve in a heavily-logged landscape. Boulder Creek Grove lacks exceptionally large specimens, but many of the trees are impressive medium-sized specimens, ten feet or more in diameter (at breast height).

Boulder Creek Grove outlier on edge of 1980s clearcut.

The abundant young sequoias along the grove's small creek show that sequoia reproduction can occur within the somewhat shady old growth forest environment though major forest clearing has not occurred. Proper germinating conditions are created when periodic floodwaters wash away the forest litter from the stream banks, exposing a bare mineral seed bed. The stream bank environment also tends to have more frequent natural, canopy-opening tree falls, and it often has more light available to young sequoias.

Well above the grove on the south, adjacent to an area clearcut in the 1980s, an exceptionally large and beautiful sequoia stands alone. Its huge crown towers over the nearby forest, so it can be seen in the distance from many locations in the Boulder Creek watershed. The U.S. Forest Service logged in this area in the 1980s, and planted sequoias afterwards. Boulder Creek Grove may expand beyond its pre-logging boundaries if these trees mature.

In a forest service survey earlier this century, the tract between the grove and the solitary sequoia mentioned above was determined to have one of the highest total conifer volumes in a non-sequoia area east of Hume Lake. Subsequent logging has erased that old-growth mixed-conifer forest spectacle, however. Even natural-appearing stands in the mixed conifer forest belt of the Sierra often are a meager indication of the old growth stands that existed before logging.

DEER MEADOW, AGNEW, AND MONARCH GROVES

Size: Small
Condition: Wilderness old growth
Management: Sequoia National Forest
Access: Cross-country (from trail to grove vicinity)

Sequoia National Forest's Deer Meadow, Agnew, and Monarch Groves are the most eastern and remote wilderness groves of the Kings River sequoia belt. They are located in rugged, vista-filled, canyon country. From the steep slopes around Deer Meadow and Agnew Groves, one overlooks Boulder Creek; to the southwest one can pick out Little Boulder Creek and Kennedy Grove, and see Evans Grove to the west. To the north are spectacular panoramas of the main Kings Canyon.

Cross-country travel is necessary to reach all of these groves, making them some of the most challenging of all groves to reach and explore. Few visit them. The best access route to the vicinity is from the Deer Meadow Ridge Trail to the east. Mapped trail access from the west is not currently recommended because a bridge washout has made crossing Boulder Creek difficult.

Deer Meadow Grove is the largest of the three. It is located on extremely steep slopes of Boulder Creek Canyon. More than sixty mature sequoias, of relatively small sizes for mature giants, are spread between 6,400 and 7,500 foot elevations. A thick population of younger "spiretop" sequoias is at the lower end of the grove, perhaps the result of an unrecorded late-nineteenth-century fire. The wildfire has created a fine example of the natural pattern of sequoia population succession in wilderness conditions.

Agnew Grove is a dense cluster of about twenty small giants on precipitous slopes in the headwaters of Rattlesnake Creek, a short distance north of Deer Meadow Grove.

Monarch Grove is a small group with about a dozen mature giants and younger sequoias, about six-tenths of a mile north of Agnew Grove in the headwaters of an unnamed minor tributary of the Kings River. It is located along the drainage, rather than on waterless slopes like Deer Meadow and Agnew Groves. This grove was the most recent of all to become identified as a separate grove; its name was adopted by Sequoia National Forest in 1996.

Agnew and Monarch Groves are in the legislated Monarch Wilderness; Deer Meadow Grove is just as wild, and may someday earn official wilderness designation.

The remote locations of these groves protected them from roads and logging, but not from fire. Located above hot, brush-covered canyon slopes, these groves have endured frequent and intense fires throughout the centuries, which probably explains the absence of many large old giants here. Still it is remarkable that some of the sequoias have survived to venerable ages in this setting.

The Deer Meadow Ridge Trail, which provides access to the vicinity of the groves, is one of the best hikes in the Hume Ranger District (though water may be scarce after early summer). After following a dirt road in a logged area to an unmarked "trailhead," the route soon climbs into unofficial wilderness, dominated by old growth red fir, with several ungrazed meadows. The trail provides vistas of the Kings Canyon country. The open granite, marked 8,644 feet in elevation on the topographic map, provides vistas east to the High Sierra; it is accessible by a short, cross-country detour from the trail. The northern extension of the trail is in the Monarch Wilderness.

Deer Meadow Grove at right center.

GROVES IN OR CONTIGUOUS
TO THE KAWEAH RIVER WATERSHED

REDWOOD MOUNTAIN GROVE 61

LOST GROVE 66

MUIR GROVE 66

SKAGWAY AND PINE RIDGE GROVES 67

SUWANEE GROVE 68

GIANT FOREST 68

CASTLE CREEK GROVE 72

REDWOOD MEADOW GROVE 74

CASE MOUNTAIN GROVE 74

ORIOLE AND NEW ORIOLE GROVES 75

EDEN CREEK GROVE 76

HORSE CREEK AND CAHOON CREEK 77
GROVES

ATWELL-EAST FORK GROVE 77

HOMERS NOSE AND 80
BOARD CAMP GROVES

SOUTH FORK GROVE 81

COFFEEPOT CANYON, SURPRISE, DEVILS 81
CANYON, AND DENNISON GROVES

GARFIELD-DILLONWOOD GROVE 82

REDWOOD MOUNTAIN GROVE

Size: Very large
Condition: Mixed
Manager: Kings Canyon National Park, Sequoia National Forest,
and University of California ("Whitaker Forest" section)
Access: Paved road and dirt road

Redwood Mountain Grove is the largest grove in total area (over
4,000 acres), has the largest area of old growth, and contains more
mature sequoias than any other grove. Though partially logged in
the 1870s, the grove also has the largest total area of unlogged
sequoia forest. Most of the grove is in the Redwood Creek drainage
of Kings Canyon National Park, which is nearly all unlogged old
growth. The grove extends to the west side of Redwood Mountain
Ridge, where most logging occurred. In that area the grove is partially managed by Sequoia National Forest and by the University of
California (the Whitaker Forest section). The grove is a contiguous
unit (except for three very small outlier groups) at elevations ranging from about 5,000 to 7,200 feet.

Highway 198 runs through the north edge of the grove, and provides a spectacular roadside vista point. The view is often marred by
hazy smog in summer. A rough dirt road from the highway descends
to the main grove trailhead at Redwood Saddle, on the boundary of
the national park and Whitaker Forest. There is a limited trail network, including several closed dirt roads. Most of the Redwood
Canyon section of the grove is trail-less wilderness. The grove has
no public facilities.

The 1968-69 sequoia inventory of only the park section of the
grove recorded 15,809 sequoias over a foot in diameter, by far the
largest number in any park grove. This included thirty-five trees at
least twenty feet in diameter at breast height (the largest being
twenty-two feet), 629 at least fifteen feet, 2,668 at least ten feet, and
5,276 at least five feet. Though a full inventory has not been done
for all the sequoia groves (or for the complete Redwood Mountain
Grove), it is almost certain that the Redwood Mountain Grove has
more large sequoias than any other grove. The park service inventory confirmed that Redwood Mountain Grove was second to
smaller Giant Forest in the total number of sequoias over fifteen feet
in diameter.

A separate inventory reported that in 1966 the Whitaker Forest
section of the grove, which suffered selective sequoia logging in the
1870s, had 228 surviving mature sequoias over eight feet in diameter (at breast height). Whitaker Forest is an example of a logged
grove section that retains impressive old growth sequoia resources.

Though large specimens are abundant, the Redwood Mountain
Grove is not known to have trees that approach record size. The
Hart Tree was once incorrectly reported to be the world's fourth
largest sequoia, but it and the nearby Roosevelt Tree are smaller

Redwood Mountain Grove.

than the top twenty trees on expert Wendell Flint's list of the largest, accurately-measured sequoias. The Hart and Roosevelt trees, the largest specimens in the grove, are located in the spectacular sequoia drainage of the East Fork of Redwood Creek, and are accessible only by trail.

Perhaps the grove's single most impressive phenomenon is the almost pure, dense stand of mature sequoias in what is known as the Sugar Bowl, on Redwood Mountain Ridge just south of the peak. This stand within a larger dense concentration of sequoias called the "Sugar Bowl Grove," is one of a very few such pure sequoia forests in the Sierra; more than fifty individuals in close proximity to the trail can be viewed from one spot there. Some have speculated that the site has the heaviest volume of wood growing on one acre of any forest in the world.

The 1987 Pierce wildfire on the west slopes of Redwood Mountain Ridge, originating on national forest land, burned into the west edges of the "Sugar Bowl Grove," killing many young sequoias and more than ten mature giants in the park. Only earlier thinning and clearing of the grove understory by park service controlled burning kept the fire from causing much worse damage. Fields of early summer lupine now grow in the hotly burned area where the fire opened the forest canopy. The fire's long-term effects will continue to be monitored.

The five-mile round trip trail to the Sugar Bowl is perhaps the most popular hike in Redwood Mountain Grove. Except for a short gap near Redwood Mountain Peak, the entire route passes through dense sequoia forest. Extensive controlled burns have been implemented in this area. The forest there now has an open, scenic character reminiscent of descriptions of Sierra forests from early explorer accounts written before twentieth century fire suppression policies.

Redwood Mountain Grove is noted for its representation of all ages of sequoias in both logged and unlogged areas. Researcher Philip Rundel concluded that it exemplified a "steady state" grove with every age of sequoia, not, as in some groves, only older or younger age classes. A study in the 1960s, which preceded extensive controlled burns, found that sequoia reproduction here was the best of any unlogged grove in Sequoia and Kings Canyon National Parks. Post-logging sequoia reproduction (most of which dates from the 1870s) is most impressive in Whitaker Forest. "Young" sequoias there, many now well over a century in age, include specimens six feet in diameter (at breast height) and over 180 feet tall. These are perhaps the oldest post-logging, regenerated sequoia stands in any grove.

From viewpoints overlooking the Redwood Canyon section, one can easily see uneven patterns of sequoia distribution within the grove. Dense concentrations such as "Sugar Bowl Grove" often seem to be "groves within groves." Aside from these localized areas of very thick sequoia growth, the grove's general sequoia density is also very high, relative to most other unlogged groves.

Looking south over Redwood Mountain Grove to Big Baldy.

View of Redwood Mountain from Highway 198.

Logging History:

The Whitaker Forest section was logged of almost all of its non-sequoia conifers and about half of its old growth sequoias between 1873 and 1879 to supply Hyde's Mill. When John Muir came across the mill in 1875, he wrote, "The mountain ridge on the south side of the stream [Redwood Mountain Ridge] was covered from base to summit with a most superb growth of Big Trees. What a picture it made! In all my forest wanderings I had seen none so sublime. . . Hyde's Mill like a bad ghost has destroyed, devoured many a fine tree from this wood. . . In this glorious forest the mill was busy, forming a sore, sad center of destruction, though small as yet, so immensely heavy was the growth."

The Hyde's Mill operation was the first major episode of old growth sequoia logging in the Sierra Nevada. Despite their destructiveness, early logging techniques were technologically restrained, compared with later practices in sites like Converse Basin and Evans Grove. Logging in Whitaker Forest predated the invention of the steam engine winch "donkey;" logs were still moved with oxen and horses. Because most cutting was done with axes rather than saws, the loggers probably selectively cut more of the smaller old growth sequoias. The surviving mature sequoias in the Whitaker Forest are larger specimens, usually ten feet or more in diameter. But the largest is only about sixteen feet in diameter (at breast height).

Whitaker Forest has been managed for preservation of old growth sequoias since it was acquired by Horace Whitaker in 1895. When the University of California obtained the land from Whitaker in 1910, it selectively logged conifers and harvested down sequoias.

Present Sequoia National Forest sections of the grove adjacent to Whitaker Forest have also been logged. Periodic forest service timber sales in and adjacent to the grove occurred up until the early 1980s, though it is believed that mature sequoias and most young sequoias were protected. Following the 1987 Pierce Fire southwest of Redwood Mountain, conifers and a minor amount of dead or damaged young sequoia were harvested in a salvage operation. The forest service now prohibits commercial logging in their section of the grove.

The grove has been a focus of fire history research. Investigators discovered that in the old growth national park sections, intense, widespread crown fires had not occurred in the past four hundred years! Research indicated that in the years between 1700 and 1875, fires happened every 30 years or less on average, and that fires were typically low intensity and small in area. This is characteristic of natural fire patterns for the entire Sierra Nevada mixed conifer zone.

Whitaker Forest was a pioneer in the Sierra Nevada controlled burn program. Controlled burning to reduce understory vegetation and debris density was commenced in the 1940s, decades before the national park prescribed burn program in groves commenced. Burning in Whitaker Forest was generally preceded by fuel removals to protect the old growth sequoias from scorching, unlike the less-protective controlled burns in the national park section of the grove that came later.

At present, more than 90% of all sequoia grove acreage is in public ownership. Of the sixty-seven groves identified in this book, thirty-seven are managed, all or in part, by the U.S. National Forest Service (primarily in the new Giant Sequoia National Monument). This is between 46% and 48% of all sequoia grove acreage. The U.S. National Park Service (at Sequoia-Kings Canyon and Yosemite National Parks) administers all or part of twenty-nine groves, including between 32% and 34% of all sequoia grove acreage.

Contrary to some past erroneous reports, most grove areas do not have the stringent protection of national park status. The giant sequoia groves in Sequoia National Forest are now protected from commercial logging by the new Giant Sequoia National Monument proclaimed by President Clinton in April 2000. Future management of these groves, however, is still largely dependent upon the administrative planning processes of the U.S. National Forest Service.

About 2% to 3% of the total grove area is on the Tule River Indian Reservation, which currently restricts public access. Private interests still own parts of ten groves. Most of the privately-held sequoia lands are small, scattered parcels. But one is a large tract in the Dillonwood section of Garfield-Dillonwood Grove. Some private holdings include exceptional sequoia resources. For example, the Stagg Tree, one of the ten largest sequoias known, is on private land in the Alder Creek Grove.

LOST GROVE

Size: Small
Condition: Old growth
Manager: Sequoia National Park
Access: Paved road

Small Lost Grove in Sequoia National Park is one of the most visited groves because Highway 198 passes right through it. It exemplifies the groves where a thick stand of majestic, towering giants can be wondered at from a main road. A short loop trail is east of (above) the parking area. Another trail through the lower part of the grove originates in Dorst Campground, to the southwest.

Sequoias are dense throughout the grove's approximately fifty acres, including many striking clusters. The 1969 National Park Service inventory counted about 130 sequoias over five feet in diameter (at breast height), including sixty-eight at least ten feet in diameter. None of the trees is a "twenty footer," though one enormously buttressed specimen beside the loop trail comes close to qualifying.

The grove has unlogged old growth, mixed-conifer forest, primarily white fir and sugar pine. As one would suspect though, you can't build a highway through a grove and preserve it at the same time. Besides the trees removed for original road construction, roadside old growth sequoias fell in 1939 and 1969, probably as a result of road construction damage. The relatively open grove understory is the result of controlled burns.

Lost Grove.

MUIR GROVE

Size: Mid-size
Condition: Wilderness old growth
Manager: Sequoia National Park
Access: Trail

Sequoia National Park's Muir Grove is one of the very finest mid-sized groves, featuring a high density of mature sequoias. Like Grant and South Calaveras Groves, its sequoia population is skewed towards the older age classes. For visitors, this means that the grove offers concentrated grandeur rarely found elsewhere. The 1969 sequoia inventory counted 814 sequoias at least five feet in diameter (at breast height), including 304 at least ten feet in diameter, and sixty at least fifteen feet in diameter. Six specimens were in the twenty to twenty-three foot diameter class.

The grove is in a beautiful wilderness setting, accessible over two miles of good trail, which continues farther through the grove. The approach and entrance to the Muir Grove are as dramatic as the visitor will encounter anywhere, making it one of the best of all day-hike grove destinations. The trailside vista from the east, across a creek gorge, to the wall of giants on the grove's edge, suggests another world. Some of the grove's finest stands are on its eastern edge, where the trail enters. The non-sequoia forest is made up primarily of white fir and sugar pine.

Looking west to Muir Grove.

A Muir Grove giant.

SKAGWAY AND PINE RIDGE GROVES

Size: Small
Condition: Wilderness old growth
Manager: Sequoia National Park
Access: Cross-country

Skagway and Pine Ridge groves are small, wilderness groves near Muir Grove, located to the south and southwest. Their sequoias occur only in moist interior drainages. Characterized as "stringer" groves, they occur in relatively narrow bands along creeks flanked by dryer slopes without sequoias. Pine Ridge Grove is one of the lowest elevation south Sierra groves, descending to about 5,600 feet. Both groves also feature old growth, mixed-conifer forest. Like most other Sequoia National Park wilderness groves, they still have not been treated with controlled fire.

The 1969 National Park Service Skagway Grove sequoia inventory counted 137 sequoias at least five feet in diameter (at breast height), including sixty-one at least ten feet in diameter (with the largest at eighteen feet). The 1969 Pine Ridge Grove inventory counted sixty-nine sequoias at least five feet in diameter (at breast height), including twenty-three at least ten feet in diameter (with the largest at nineteen feet). Both groves have good populations of younger sequoias.

These groves are not visible from Highway 198. Skagway once had trail access from Muir Grove, but that trail became overgrown after maintenance ceased. Ironically, Sequoia National Park had more maintained trails in the 1930s than it does today. Several park groves like Skagway, once reached by trail, are now only accessible by difficult, unsigned cross-country travel. Though not isolated by great distances, Skagway and Pine Ridge Groves are "remote" in practical terms because they lack good trail access. Visitors are assured of solitude.

SUWANEE GROVE

Size: Small
Condition: Old growth
Manager: Sequoia National Park
Access: Cross-country

Suwanee Grove is one of the finest small groves. It enjoys a spectacular setting of old growth wilderness forest, perched on the rim of the canyon of the Marble Fork of the Kaweah River (which canyon separates it from Giant Forest to the south). An old trail to the grove was abandoned. It now is reached by a few miles of cross-country forest travel over relatively easy terrain.

For its size, the grove has a remarkable number of exceptionally large specimens; its mature sequoia population is older and larger than that of a typical grove. The 1969 sequoia inventory counted 176 sequoias at least five feet in diameter (at breast height), including seventy-nine at least ten feet in diameter. Three specimens were over twenty feet in diameter, and one snag relic of an enormous sequoia had a diameter of twenty-five feet (probably without bark and sapwood). The grove is in an extremely fine mixed-conifer area, sprinkled with enormous sugar pines.

The grove now has a relatively open understory and lower risk of destructive wildfire, as a result of park service controlled burns in the early 1990s.

GIANT FOREST

Size: Large
Condition: Old growth
Manager: Sequoia National Park
Access: Paved road

Giant Forest is probably the most famous single grove of sequoias. Not only is it the largest of the unlogged groves, it contains more exceptionally large sequoias over fifteen and twenty feet in diameter (at breast height) than any other grove. It is also home to the largest living sequoia, the General Sherman Tree. The threat of logging in the Giant Forest was the major impetus for the 1890 creation of Sequoia National Park, which also protected numerous other groves.

Giant Forest is located on a generally rolling plateau between the merging canyons of the Marble and Middle Forks of the Kaweah River. Like a storybook "lost world," Giant Forest is naturally isolated by deep canyons on three sides and a ridge on the east.

The General Sherman Tree.

Sequoias spill off the plateau and descend downslope some distance into the Marble Fork drainage. Except for two small western outlier groups, the grove is a contiguous unit of many lobes, once described as "scores of groves merging into one another." It sits in an uneven-aged old growth mixed conifer forest, where white firs and sugar pines are most common.

The grove boasts exceptionally easy access and developed tourist facilities nearby. Highway 198, the "General's Highway" (so named because it connects the General Grant and the General Sherman Trees), goes through the grove. A paved, but winding and narrow road also runs through the grove, leading to the granite viewpoint at Moro Rock and to Crescent Meadow, where the High Sierra Trail to Mount Whitney takes off. The grove has a more extensive network of maintained trails than any other grove.

The first of the comprehensive sequoia inventories for Sequoia and Kings Canyon National Park groves was undertaken in 1964 at Giant Forest. It counted eighty-six specimens at least twenty feet in diameter (at breast height), 779 at least fifteen feet, 2,571 at least ten feet, and 5,356 at least five feet. The grove is unsurpassed for its number of twenty-foot or larger sequoias, having more than twice as many as its nearest competitor for that distinction, Redwood Mountain Grove. Only logged Converse Basin Grove may have surpassed it in total number of exceptionally large specimens.

When all of the over-twenty-foot-diameter trees inventoried in Sequoia and Kings Canyon Parks are aggregated, Giant Forest alone has almost half of them. Other Giant Forest statistics are similarly impressive. The grove includes four of the five largest known sequoias (in total volume), and an unusually high percentage of the grove's sequoias reach exceptionally large sizes. The Giant Forest count showed that 14.5% of its trees at least five feet in diameter (at breast height) and 30.3% of its sequoias at least ten feet in diameter

Left: Crown of the Franklin Tree in Giant Forest.

Right: The Washington Tree in Giant Forest.

Giant sequoia log in Giant Forest.

were also at least fifteen feet in diameter.

Giant Forest is also noted for its many dense groups of spectacu-lar old growth sequoias, such as the Founders, House, and Senate Groups (all on the Congress Trail). Sequoia scholar Philip Rundel's studies showed that Giant Forest, like Redwood Mountain Grove, is a "steady-state" grove, with a substantially blended mix of all sequoia age classes.

The General Sherman Tree, at the northwest edge of the grove, is the world's largest living tree by far. The Sherman is a short walk from an often-jammed parking lot by Highway 198. In 1981, the tree was measured to be about 275 feet high, with a ground perime-ter of 102.6 feet, diameters of 21.6 feet (at 16 feet above ground) and a remarkable 17.3 feet (at 120 feet above ground), and a vol-ume of about 52,500 cubic feet (ignoring burns). The Sherman has a 10 to 12 percent greater volume than the second and third largest known sequoias, the Washington Tree of Giant Forest and the General Grant Tree of Grant Grove.

Though not the largest sequoia at its base, the Sherman is unri-valed among the largest class of sequoias in overall lack of taper in the ascending trunk. It may be the world's fastest growing tree in terms of added volume, based on comparative measurements made in 1931 and 1975. As of 1975, its largest branch started 130 feet up the trunk, had a basal diameter of nearly seven feet, and was 125 feet long.

The Washington Tree is the second largest known tree, despite a badly damaged top (reducing it to about 246 feet high). The Washington would have the greatest diameter at breast height of a living sequoia (26 feet) if a buttress of the General Grant Tree was ignored. The Washington is even a bit thicker than the Sherman at 16 feet above the ground.

The President Tree, on the Congress Trail, is the fourth largest known tree. It has been described as having "the most rugged branches" (up to eight feet in diameter) of any Giant Forest sequoia. The Lincoln Tree is the fifth largest known tree.

Until recently devastated by lightning, the Soldiers' Trail Tree was distinctive among the "top twenty" size specimens for its minimal mid-trunk taper. The column-like giant narrowed only about half a foot in diameter from the 60-foot level to the 180-foot level, and just more than one foot in diameter from 60 to 210.5 feet. It was thicker than the General Sherman Tree for that part of its height above about 185 feet.

The grove is also notable for a trove of dead sequoia remnants. The sequoia inventory counted 1,193 dead, fallen, or stump sequoias. Many of these relics are as impressive in size as living spec-imens. The inventory identified 74 snags over 15 feet in diameter, including 16 over 20 feet, with the largest at 26 feet). "Old One Hundred," a large burned snag near Circle Meadow, has been dated to have lived about 3,100 years. Large sequoias fall from natural causes each decade in Giant Forest.

Despite the grove's plethora of named trees, a 1986 National Park Service report recommended that grove interpretation focus on forest ecology and not on "oddities" like named trees. It referred to Giant Forest features such as the drive-through Auto Log with disdain, and referred to named trees as "quaint reminders of the past."

The grove is the only one of the largest groves that was spared from commercial logging. Its status as a national park, however, has not guaranteed full protection for the Giant Forest. Use by millions of visitors over time has had a telling effect on this once-virgin landscape.

Giant Forest, with its major human impacts, has presented continuing management challenges. From the time road access was completed in 1903 until the 1950s, sections of the grove experienced disruption from a "camping chaos" of "ramshackle temporary structures." Campgrounds and many structures were removed from within the grove before the 1990s. In 1999, the park service completed the process of relocating the park's primary commercial lodging from Giant Forest to Wuksachi Village, eight miles to the north. Most structures in Giant Forest have been demolished, and their sites are being restored to natural conditions. A museum (to open in 2001) and related day-use facilities will remain. Giant Forest has become the best example of a grove where once-major developments have been almost entirely removed. Auto impacts are also being reduced by introduction of a free shuttle service between Giant Forest and the Wuksachi Village area. The shuttle will also go to Moro Rock and Crescent Meadow.

Historically, grazing in Giant Forest was remarkable for its intensity. After Hale Tharp became the first non-Native American to discover the grove, he set up a cattle ranch there. During the severe drought year of 1864, four thousand cattle grazed in Giant Forest. The grove suffered regular grazing in and around private ranch inholdings from the 1870s to the 1920s.

Spectacular Moro Rock, a granite dome on the south edge of the grove, above the Middle Fork Kaweah Canyon, provides a classic High Sierra vista of Great Western Divide peaks to the east, as well as panoramic views of the Middle Fork Canyon and the grove rim. Beetle Rock and Sunset Rock also are outstanding viewpoints.

Grove giants grow to the edge of precipices above the canyons of the Marble and Middle Forks, adding to the grove's "other world" quality. The grove is known for the number and area of its many beautiful meadows such as Log, Round, Circle, Huckleberry, and Crescent. The grove is unrivaled among unlogged groves for its total meadow area. Crescent Meadow and Log Meadow are each more than a half-mile long.

The grove has been the site of extensive controlled fires since 1979 for the primary purpose of fire hazard reduction. About 1,200 acres have experienced such burns. Because of its location within a national park, the grove is a perfect "laboratory" for study of the effects of controlled fires.

The Giant Forest burn program has been the subject of much scientific and political scrutiny. Some of the pre-1986 fires provoked public outcry that the burns were too severe and carelessly administered. Critics asserted that the fires charred sequoia trunks as high as fifty feet and killed some mature pine and fir, thus seriously diminishing grove scenic qualities. The fires destroyed the Tunnel Log, a popular sequoia feature that fell in 1937. Controlled burns

Circle Meadow in Giant Forest.

The Lincoln Tree in Giant Forest.

also may have killed some living old growth sequoias that were particularly vulnerable due to old fire scars or other factors.

In response to this criticism, the park service temporarily suspended controlled burning in 1986 and later resumed burning under new guidelines. These new guidelines were developed by an independent panel of experts who reviewed the grove burning controversies. The panel recognized that scenic considerations are important in the parks, but it firmly reinforced the park service's express policy of allowing natural processes to continue. It noted that sequoia groves, with the exception of developed and "showcase" areas, are not forest "museums" that can be frozen in time. The group suggested that generally, scenic considerations should be secondary to maintaining or simulating natural processes, when it comes to controlled burning. However, the panel recommended that the burning program provide special protection of sequoias from controlled burn scorching in several high-visitation areas within Giant Forest.

The appearance of burned areas in Giant Forest is improving, with the fall of many small, fire-killed trees. The charring and scorching of sequoias from prescribed burns (that prompted criticism in the 1980s) are now largely gone. Superficially charred sequoia bark harmlessly flakes off within several years.

As of 1991, the hazard reduction burn program for natural areas of Giant Forest was essentially finished. Follow-up burns will be undertaken when fuel loads again accumulate to fire hazard level (perhaps in fifteen to twenty years). It is expected that eventually fire management will consist primarily of monitored, but unsuppressed, natural lightning fires rather than controlled fires.

CASTLE CREEK GROVE

Size: Mid-size
Condition: Wilderness old growth
Manager: Sequoia National Park
Access: Cross-country

Castle Creek Grove is a remote, trail-less, mid-sized wilderness grove in Sequoia National Park. It is distributed in four units along forks of Castle Creek, in the Middle Fork of the Kaweah River drainage. Though not distant from trailheads, the grove is only accessible by very difficult cross-country travel.

This grove was not historically used by Native Americans, and it has little modern human visitation. The 1969 NPS sequoia inventory counted 382 trees at least 5 feet in diameter (at breast height), including 133 at least 10 feet in diameter, as well as numerous younger sequoias, in the old-growth, mixed-conifer forest. Like many "canyon" groves, vulnerable to more frequent intense fires, it lacks many exceptionally large specimens. In the lower reaches of the grove, sequoias occur down to 4,900 feet, unusually low for the southern Sierra.

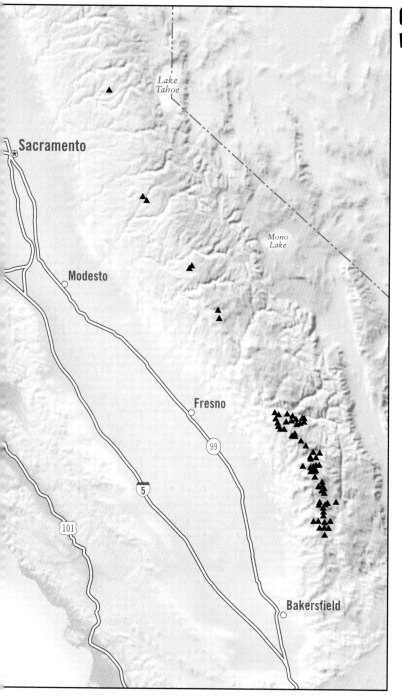

Sequoias are distributed in a small number of isolated concentrations, traditionally called "groves," in a narrow strip less than twenty miles wide on the west slope of the Sierra Nevada. They extend from Placer County Grove in the American River drainage on the north, to Deer Creek Grove, about 250 miles to the south. Authorities and public agencies differ in their identifications of groves, partly because criteria for defining a distinct grove can vary. This book identifies sixty-seven groves.

The eight groves that occur north of the Kings River are spread over 160 miles. Placer County Grove is both the northernmost and the most isolated grove. North Calaveras Grove, its nearest neighbor, is sixty miles south. The reasons for wide gaps between some northern groves are unknown.

The fifty-nine southern groves are irregularly distributed within a sixty-mile stretch. In this southern sequoia range, no one grove is remote from another, and in some areas groves are close enough that they are considered an "interrupted belt."

Sequoias naturally occur on an infinitesimal fraction of the earth's forested surface. The sequoia groves aggregate only about 36,000 to 38,000 acres in total area. Much of this acreage has been logged to some extent since the 1870s, so the total amount of unlogged grove land is considerably smaller. The global rarity of old growth sequoia forest cannot be overstated.

Within the time frame of the last 10,000 years or so, it is not understood why sequoia groves occur only where they do. It is also perplexing that sequoias do not occur naturally in apparently suitable Sierra Nevada forest sites where they often prosper when planted.

REDWOOD MEADOW GROVE

Size: Mid-size
Condition: Wilderness old growth
Manager: Sequoia National Park
Access: Trail

Dogwood in autumn.

Redwood Meadow Grove is a mid-sized wilderness grove complex of two main units plus small outlying sequoia groups in the upper Middle Fork of the Kaweah River watershed. It is the most eastern Sequoia National Park grove, and one of the finest and most varied of wilderness groves. The 1976 sequoia inventory counted 594 sequoias at least 5 feet in diameter (at breast height), including 246 at least 10 feet in diameter and three specimens 20 feet in diameter. The grove is characterized by an unusually high number of younger sequoias, many of which regenerated after major fires in the 1870s. The abundant twenty to twenty-five year old post-fire sequoias that pioneer forester George Sudworth observed in 1900 are now well over a century old. Past fires also left a number of large, dead, old-growth sequoias, both standing and down.

The two main grove units have many fine sequoias, but the groups vary in character. The larger "Redwood Meadow" unit has good trail access from Middle Fork trailheads and from the Atwell trailhead to the south. Much of the grove, however, is accessible only by cross-country travel. The Redwood Meadow unit has old growth mixed conifer forest and abundant water. The smaller, waterless "Little Redwood Meadow" unit can only be reached cross-country. It is untypically set within a red fir forest.

The grove has been recognized among the many Sequoia National Park roadless groves as one of the priority areas for controlled fire treatment.

CASE MOUNTAIN GROVE

Size: Small
Condition: Mixed
Manager: Bureau of Land Management and private owners
Access: Trail (closed dirt road)

Case Mountain Grove is a remote complex of three small groups with surviving old growth sequoias on Bureau of Land Management (B.L.M.) land, and a larger, adjacent area still in private ownership. The private grove land was logged of nearly all old growth sequoias by the early 1950s. That logged area is home to many young sequoias, both naturally regenerated and planted.

An estimated 90 to 100 sequoias at least 5 feet in diameter (at breast height), including about 40 specimens at least 10 feet in diameter, occur on the public grove land. None are exceptionally large. Extremely vigorous stands of young sequoia indicate that the grove is an excellent sequoia growing site. Nearly all of the old-growth non-sequoia conifers have been logged.

Documentation concerning numbers of logged old growth sequoias is lacking, but it is estimated that perhaps 25 to 30 trees

Dogwood in autumn.

were cut in one of the last excesses of private sequoia logging.

The publicly-owned section of the grove is unique for being the only site managed by the B.L.M. Though the grove is adjacent to Sequoia National Park, because of a quirk the park service never sought to acquire it. Current B.L.M. policy is to preserve the grove from further logging. As of 1999, there was no public vehicle access. There are no plans to acquire private land in the grove at this time.

The B.L.M.-managed portion of the grove may slowly revert to a wilderness condition. The grove is in a high fire hazard area, on steep slopes above brushy lower slopes. A major fire in 1987 toppled one old growth sequoia.

ORIOLE AND NEW ORIOLE GROVES

Size: Oriole is small; New Oriole is tiny
Condition: Wilderness old growth
Manager: Sequoia National Park
Access: Cross-country

Oriole Grove is a Sequoia National Park wilderness grove that, like Muir and Suwanee Groves, is extremely impressive for its size. Its mature sequoia population consists mainly of older, larger trees. The 1969 sequoia inventory showed that Oriole Grove's slightly more than 100 acres encompassed 362 trees at least 5 feet in diameter (at breast height), including 176 at least 10 feet in diameter. Exceptionally large sequoias over 15 feet in diameter are common, and 3 specimens were 20 feet in diameter or greater. Grove sequoias occur over an elevation range of more than 1,500 feet in a long and narrow band along Squirrel Creek, amidst fine old growth, mixed-conifer forest, with some red fir at the upper edge.

An old access trail to the Oriole Grove was abandoned by the National Park Service (like several other Sequoia National Park grove access trails). The cross-country hike in is short but challenging.

Strenuous cross-country travel through old growth, mixed-conifer forest is necessary to reach the very small New Oriole Grove, about three-quarters of a mile south of Oriole Grove along a small tributary of Squirrel Creek. Though only about 10 acres in size, this wilderness grove had 39 sequoias at least 5 feet in diameter (at breast height), including 15 at least 10 feet in diameter (with the largest reaching 17 feet) in 1969. The grove is at the relatively low elevation of about 5,900 feet. Visitors there are assured of solitude.

EDEN CREEK GROVE

Size: Mid-size
Condition: Wilderness old growth
Manager: Sequoia National Park
Access: Cross-country

Eden Creek Grove is the largest and one of the least-visited of the trail-less wilderness groves in Sequoia National Park. The 1975 sequoia inventory counted 856 sequoias at least 5 feet in diameter (at breast height), including 351 at least 10 feet in diameter. A total of 55 giants were from 15 to 20 feet in diameter. The sequoias are scattered, with most concentrated along the several forks of Eden Creek, tributary to the East Fork of the Kaweah River. Some can be spotted from the Mineral King Road (at a distance to the south), but most are in inner drainages and obscured from view.

It is somewhat surprising that this virtually-unknown, mid-sized grove has significantly more large sequoias than famous groves like North Calaveras and Mariposa. With so many sequoias and as a preserve for extensive stands of old growth, mixed conifers, Eden Creek Grove has biological significance that far surpasses its renown.

The grove is naturally highly susceptible to fire, a condition that has been severely aggravated by twentieth-century fire suppression. Its overgrown understory could help generate an intensely destructive crown fire that might kill many old growth giants; steps need to be taken to reduce accumulated woody fuels.

Access to the grove is by arduous cross-country "bushwhacking," a fact that ensures that the grove will remain one of the least-visited forest "Edens" in the Sierra. Because of hazards associated with the remote and rugged conditions, and due to high fire danger, the N.P.S. does not encourage grove exploration by the average visitor. The Eden Creek Grove is only for the most capable and resolute adventurer.

HORSE CREEK AND CAHOON CREEK GROVES

Size: Small
Condition: Wilderness old growth
Manager: Sequoia National Park
Access: Cross-country

East of Eden Creek Grove in the extremely rugged and trail-less wilderness canyon terrain of the East Fork of the Kaweah River drainage, are small Horse Creek and Cahoon Creek Groves. These creekside "stringer" groves are close together, separated by a ridge between Horse Creek and its tributary Cahoon Creek. Access requires difficult cross-country hiking, and visitors should be prepared to deal with the risks of remoteness and high fire hazard.

Like many canyon groves, these lack exceptionally large sequoias. But there is much to appreciate here for those who seek out remote forest wonders. The 1975 NPS sequoia inventory counted 108 sequoias at least 5 feet in diameter (at breast height), including 34 at least 10 feet in diameter (the largest being 16 feet) along Horse Creek. Smaller Cahoon Creek Grove had 35 sequoias at least 5 feet in diameter, including 18 at least 10 feet in diameter.

ATWELL-EAST FORK GROVE

Size: Very large
Condition: Mixed, but primarily wilderness old growth
Manager: Sequoia National Park
Access: Paved road

The Atwell-East Fork Grove is the second largest grove (in total area) within Sequoia and Kings Canyon National Parks, exceeded in size only by Redwood Mountain Grove. It is one of the most expansive and magnificent groves of the Sierra, with more than 1,600 giants at least 10 feet in diameter (at breast height). Sequoias are spread abundantly on both slopes of the East Fork Kaweah River canyon, from the river's edge to the highest elevation of any grove in the Atwell section.

The greater grove complex traditionally has been identified as two or three separate groves. Different sections were named "Atwell Grove" (the large, partially logged site north of the East Fork of the Kaweah River), "East Fork Grove" (a sizable, generally unlogged group along and south of the East Fork, which includes a small east unit), and "Redwood Creek Grove" (a small, creekside stringer segment just west of the main Atwell section). Because these three "groves" are separated by only a few hundred yards at most, however, they have been joined together here as units of a single large grove. The traditional names are still a good way to describe the grove sections. Elevations range from 5,300 (East Fork section) to 8,800 feet (in the Atwell unit), the highest elevation for any naturally-occurring sequoia.

With acquisition by the N.P.S. of large private parcels in the East Fork section in 1986, nearly the entire grove is included in Sequoia

Atwell-East Fork Grove.

National Park. The Mineral King Road goes through the Redwood Creek and lower Atwell sections. Most of the grove has no facilities, though there are rental cabins and other visitor services at the Silver City private inholding, just east of the Atwell section of the grove. There are a few trails, but broader grove exploration, particularly in the East Fork and Redwood Creek sections, requires cross-country travel over steep and rugged terrain.

The Atwell unit suffered irregular, partial logging of its sequoias and other old growth between 1879 and 1920, before park acquisition, and some of the grove's largest sequoias were cut. The Atwell Mill Campground is filled with tall sequoia stumps. Fortunately, the grove's remoteness kept logging at a relatively low level, and most of the old growth survived.

In 1891, the small Atwell Mill was briefly leased by the utopian-socialist Kaweah colonists, after their logging operations at Colony Mill near Giant Forest were terminated by the creation of Sequoia National Park. Initial efforts of the U.S. Army to evict the colonists from their new Atwell Mill site were stopped by court injunction. However, the colony effectively disbanded anyway by 1892. Some ancient sequoias were logged in the 1950s on a since-acquired private inholding—one of the last instances when old growth sequoias were cut.

Most of the grove (including nearly the entire East Fork section) is wilderness, filled with old growth sequoia forest. Despite its logging history, the Atwell unit retains the largest number of mature sequoias in the grove, and the largest specimens. The 1969 inventory listed 22 sequoias at least 20 feet in diameter (at breast height), with the largest at 22 feet, 290 at least 15 feet, 1,072 at least 10 feet, and 2,253 at least 5 feet. In the entire Sierra, only Giant Forest and Redwood Mountain Groves have more exceptionally large specimens 18 or more feet in diameter. The unlogged sections of the Atwell unit have a relatively large proportion of ancient specimens, while maintaining the character of an "all-aged" sequoia population. The once-logged parts of the Atwell unit feature vigorous stands of maturing younger sequoias (up to 100 years old or more), intermingled with durable old growth stumps. A curiosity of the Atwell unit is a branch 12 feet in diameter (perhaps the largest of any tree in the world) discovered by sequoia expert Wendell Flint.

The western section of the largely unlogged East Fork unit has a superabundance of younger sequoias that have grown during the last 150 years following fires and avalanches. The same western section is also remarkable for having one of the highest densities of large sequoias in an unlogged grove area. The 1969 park service inventory of most of the East Fork section cataloged one tree that was 20 feet in diameter (at breast height), 83 trees at least 15 feet, 441 at least 10 feet, and 1,009 at least 5 feet. U.S. Forest Service and private land in the East Fork section, later added to the park, includes several hundred more mature sequoias.

In the Redwood Creek unit, the 1969 sequoia inventory showed 105 trees at least 5 feet in diameter (at breast height), including 46 sequoias at least 10 feet. One specimen was 21 feet in diameter.

The Atwell and Redwood Creek portions of the grove, above the

Opposite and above: Atwell-East Fork Grove.

Mineral King Road, had a widespread controlled burn in 1995. This reduced the fire hazard there and opened up the understory.

From vistas along the Mineral King Road, the East Fork unit appears as an unbroken, dense forest. This was not always so, even in recent history. A few conspicuous clusters of tall sequoia snags suggest the area's fire history. Heavy fires in 1893 and 1916 reportedly divided the main East Fork unit into two forest areas separated by a ridge covered only with chaparral and scattered trees. But in the more than 80 years since the last major fire, the area has recovered a vigorous, unbroken forest character.

Except for areas of younger trees in logged parts of the Atwell unit and in parts of the main East Fork unit that burned in this century, the grove forest is primarily mixed-conifer old growth. Where the grove reaches relatively high elevations both north and south of the East Fork, the sequoias also grow with red fir. As one would expect, studies indicate that some sequoias from this grove have genetically evolved to be more tolerant of cold extremes than sequoias in most other groves.

HOMERS NOSE AND BOARD CAMP GROVES

Size: Small
Condition: Wilderness old growth
Manager: Sequoia National Park
Access: Cross-country

Homers Nose and Board Camp Groves are two small Sequoia National Park wilderness groves on the south-facing canyon slopes of the sequoia-laden drainage of the South Fork of the Kaweah River. The groves are close to each other; Homers Nose Grove, named for a prominent knob on the ridgetop above the grove, sits just over a narrow ridge from the considerably smaller Board Camp Grove, on the east. An unmaintained trail accesses the lower edge of Homers Nose Grove, but further exploration of the groves must be done on foot and cross-country.

Most of the Homers Nose Grove sequoias, including all of the larger specimens, are broadly scattered in the upper basin of Cedar Creek. The grove extends downstream in a narrow stringer configuration, and includes a dense population of young sequoias in a small area at the grove's lowest elevation. The 1975 Homers Nose inventory listed 286 sequoias at least 5 feet in diameter (at breast height), with 109 at least 10 feet (the largest being 19 feet). Smaller Board Camp Grove had 86 sequoias at least 5 feet in diameter, including 31 over 10 feet. The sequoia populations of both groves are predominantly young, though there are several exceptionally large trees. The associated forest is old growth, mixed-conifer.

The sequoia with the largest diameter in the Board Camp Grove inventory adapted to its steep site by developing a freakishly large base. Though the tree does not approach record size, rumors of an enormous, record-breaking "Homers Nose Tree" have circulated since the nineteenth century. This remarkable individual exemplifies the wonderful variety of trees that grove explorers can search out in their wanderings.

SOUTH FORK GROVE

Size: Mid-size
Type: Wilderness old growth
Manager: Sequoia National Park
Access: Cross country

South Fork Grove is a fine mid-sized wilderness grove, east of Homers Nose and Board Camp Groves. Unlike those groves to the west and above, South Fork Grove extends along the banks of the South Fork of the Kaweah River, spreading up the canyon slopes. The grove is accessible cross-country over a route along the South Fork.

The 1975 sequoia inventory reported that there were 432 South Fork sequoias at least 5 feet in diameter (at breast height), including 167 at least 10 feet. Three specimens were at least 20 feet in diameter. The associated forest is old growth, mixed-conifer. Despite its outstanding sequoia attractions, the grove is little visited.

COFFEEPOT CANYON, SURPRISE, DEVILS CANYON, AND DENNISON GROVES

Size: Tiny
Type: Wilderness old growth
Manager: Sequoia National Park
Access: Cross-country

Coffeepot Canyon, Surprise, Devils Canyon, and Dennison are small, remote groves with much in common. They don't contain large numbers of sequoias, are set in old growth, mixed-conifer forest, are located in a wilderness section of Sequoia National Park, and are virtually inaccessible because of the nearly prohibitive amount of steep, cross-country bushwhacking required to reach them. Few hikers have visited them since the National Park Service inventoried their sequoias in the 1970s.

Coffeepot Canyon and Surprise Groves have the fewest large sequoias of any of the groves in Sequoia National Park; each has a total of less than 10 sequoias at least 10 feet in diameter (at breast height), plus smaller specimens. Surprise Grove is so small that it is debatable whether it deserves the title of "grove" at all. But it gains that recognition because of its natural occurrence remote from other groves.

The sequoias of Devils Canyon and Dennison Groves are generally old and large. Devils Canyon Grove (6 acres) has 17 specimens at least 10 feet in diameter (at breast height) with the largest 18 feet in diameter; Dennison Grove (10 acres) has 15 specimens at least 10 feet in diameter (largest 17 feet). Dennison Grove, at the southwest corner of the park, is actually in the drainage of the North Fork of the Tule River, but it is grouped with the Kaweah River watershed groves because of its proximity and similarity to them. If the groves weren't so inaccessible, they would be attractive hiking destinations.

GARFIELD-DILLONWOOD GROVE

Size: Large
Type: Mixed
Manager: Garfield section: Sequoia National Park; Dillonwood section: primarily in private ownership, with some area managed by Sequoia National Forest
Access: Garfield section: trail and cross-country; Dillonwood section: cross-country, with no public access to private section

Garfield-Dillonwood Grove is one of the very largest in area, and almost surely ranks in the top five groves in total number of mature and old growth sequoias. The Garfield section in Sequoia National Park is one of the most magnificent wilderness grove areas.

The grove has two sections that contrast greatly in condition. These sections were traditionally identified as separate "Garfield" and "Dillonwood" groves. But these sequoia areas are contiguous and more reasonably recognized as sections of a single grove. In contrast to the public forest wilderness of the Garfield section, the Dillonwood section has been heavily logged, and it is still largely in private hands.

The grove is located on the steep slopes north and south of Dennison Ridge, which forms the divide between the South Fork of the Kaweah River and the North Fork of the Tule River. Originally, the trees in the northern (Kaweah) drainage were referred to as the "Garfield Grove" and those in the Tule drainage section as the "Dillonwood Grove," though "Garfield Grove" evolved to refer to the entire section within Sequoia National Park (including the upper reaches of the grove in the Tule River drainage).

The grove grandly spreads over a range of about 3,000 feet, from near the South Fork of the Kaweah River at an unusually low grove elevation of about 4,600 feet, up the Dennison Ridge to about 7,600 feet. Several young sequoias, at some distance from the main grove, occur down to about 2,700 feet along the South Fork to the west and are thought to be the lowest naturally occurring sequoia specimens. They probably were seeded when 1867 floodwaters floated sequoia logs far downstream.

The Garfield section is accessible by about three miles of unremittingly steep trail from the end of the South Fork Road. Most of that vast grove can only be explored by difficult cross-country travel. Sequoia National Forest sections of the Dillonwood Grove, primarily east of the private land, are also trail-less. The privately owned Dillonwood section has dirt road access, but no present public access.

The sequoias in the Garfield section are spectacular and abundant. The 1974 inventory of sequoias on Sequoia National Park

Redwood cones and foliage: giant sequoia at right; coast redwood at left.

The giant sequoia *(Sequoiadendron giganteum)* is related to the coast redwood *(Sequoia sempervirens)*, but it is botanically distinct. Past names for the giant sequoia include "Big Tree," "redwood," and "Sierra redwood," but the tree is now commonly called "sequoia." Now "redwood" generally refers to coast redwood.

Aside from physical characteristics, the simple way to distinguish coast redwood and giant sequoia is geographically. The sequoia has a very limited, non-continuous distribution of less than 40,000 acres in the mountainous Sierra Nevada of California. Coast redwood occurs over more than 1.5 million acres at relatively low elevations along the north coast of California (from Monterey County north to just over the Oregon border), including large areas of continuous redwood forest.

Another conspicuous distinction between sequoias and coast redwood is their growth forms. Old growth sequoias rarely top 300 feet, in contrast to the coast redwood, the tallest North American conifer. Several coast redwoods are now over 360 feet tall. Mature sequoias, however, typically develop a much larger diameter and total size than mature coast redwoods. A large old growth sequoia will often have about double the total trunk volume of a typical large old growth coast redwood. Very few coast redwoods attain a girth of even fifteen feet in diameter (at breast height), but thousands of sequoias are that size or larger.

land listed 9 trees over 20 feet in diameter (at breast height), 290 at least 15 feet, 1,324 at least 10 feet, and 3,074 at least 5 feet. The King Arthur Tree, measured to be about 270 feet tall, and with one of the largest basal ground perimeters of any of the near-record size sequoias (about 104 feet), may be the tenth largest sequoia. It grows on a slope of about 30 degrees, illustrating that huge sequoias do not occur only in gentle-sloped terrain.

The great majority of old growth sequoias were logged on the private Dillonwood section, but that section retains about 100 mature sequoias. In addition, perhaps 50 or more old growth sequoias survive in the adjacent Sequoia National Forest on the fringes of the Dillonwood private parcel, primarily east of the North Fork of the Tule River. The private Dillonwood section also has extensive, vigorous stands of young and mid-aged sequoias that have grown since logging in the 1880s, including specimens up to 6 feet in diameter.

The logged Dillonwood landscape has recovered its appearance as a scenic forest less than fifty years after the end of the last intensive logging. Current private owners have allowed the forest to reestablish itself. Given another century or two, the Dillonwood section should regain an old growth forest character, much like the Garfield section, if it is protected from resumption of intensive logging.

The non-sequoia forest in the Garfield section is primarily old growth, mixed-conifer, with some red fir in the upper grove. The Dillonwood section has the same forest mix, but is dominated by younger, post-logging conifers, though there are a few old growth patches in Sequoia National Forest areas east and west of the private land.

Before the Dillonwood section was logged, the Garfield-Dillonwood Grove probably had more mature sequoias than Giant Forest, which would have made it the third or fourth largest original grove in number of mature sequoias, and in a class with the Redwood Mountain, Converse Basin, and Mountain Home Groves.

Logging History

The Dillonwood private lands have an unfortunate and ironic two-stage sequoia logging history. First, the grove was logged sporadically and selectively from about 1875 to 1914. Then, after more than three decades of respite, the grove was intensively logged again between 1948 and 1958.

About 1875, Nathan Dillon started logging in the grove area before the land was surveyed; at that time there was no regulation of logging on this public land. After private acquisition of public timberlands became feasible following 1878 legislation, Dillon obtained about 1,000 acres in the lower grove. The Dillon Mill handled trees logged in a non-intensive, selective manner from about 1875 to 1900. Timber was transported from the woods to the mill by an unusual wooden-rail railroad, that utilized gravity to move logs to the mill, and livestock teams to pull empty cars back upslope to the logging sites.

Many large sequoias were cut before 1914. Pioneer dendrochronologist Ellsworth Huntington studied tree rings of Dillonwood sequoia stumps in 1911-12, finding 21 specimens over 1,000 years old, and 3 over 2,000 years of age (in a limited sampling). The early logging was selective, however, and many old growth sequoias at lower elevations were spared. The upper reaches of the Dillonwood section were not logged then.

From 1948 to 1958, an industrial logging enterprise acquired and intensively logged the remaining primeval sequoia forest of Dillonwood. The old growth sequoia losses have not been documented, but they are indicated by reports such as that of the National Geographic Society, which reported 200 sequoias (including exceptionally large specimens) cut in one year.

Unfortunately, the old growth resources of Dillonwood were never inventoried or studied in any detail before the logging. That leaves Dillonwood as one of the least appreciated and understood of the large grove areas. It almost certainly had more old growth sequoias than some famous N.P.S. groves, such as the Mariposa Grove in Yosemite. For reasons difficult to understand, the National Park Service never sought to acquire the Dillonwood area after Sequoia National Park was created in 1890. The surviving Dillonwood sequoias should have been publicly acquired by the 1930s, when most of the other remaining privately-held sequoias in the Sierra were acquired.

One of the most cataclysmic events affecting the Sierra Nevada in historic times impacted the Garfield section of the grove. On December 20, 1867, a warm rain fell on heavy snowpack blanketing the higher elevations of Dennison Ridge. One observer wrote that "the north side of Dennison Mountain" fell through the heart of the grove into the South Fork of the Kaweah, destroying a reported one-third of the grove's forest. The avalanche and landslide swept down from as high as 7,500 feet, covering hundreds of acres, and devastating an area about 2.5 miles long and ranging in width from 1,500 to 4,000 feet. A natural dam was created measuring a half-mile wide and 400 feet high, and the reservoir that formed behind it breached the dam on Christmas night.

The flood scoured the canyon, then flooded Visalia in the Central Valley to a depth of five feet. Sequoia logs and tree sections were carried to the valley, where they floated far and wide beyond the riverbanks. Though new growth has disguised most signs of the 1867 avalanche in the grove, its effects are still dramatically apparent in the vicinity of Snowslide Canyon, where dense sequoia forest ends abruptly at an avalanche boulder field which swept away all that was growing there before the slide.

A 1985 controlled fire (the first in a national park roadless grove) and an unsuppressed 1986 lightning fire burned a total of about 300 acres in the central grove, including areas adjacent to the grove trail.

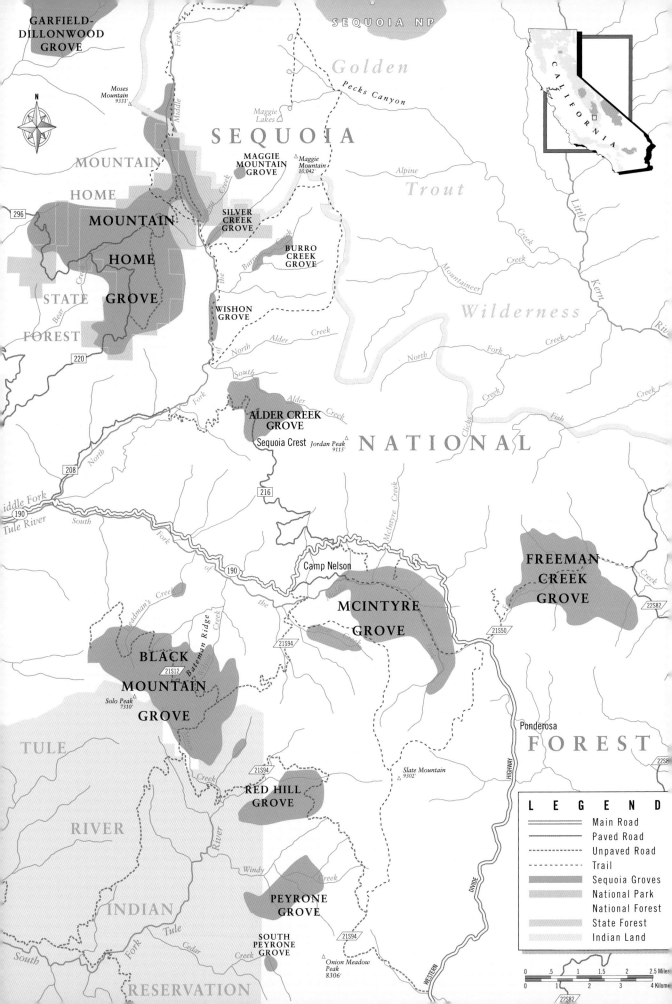

GARFIELD-
DILLONWOOD
GROVE

SEQUOIA NP

Golden

Pecks Canyon

SEQUOIA

Moses
Mountain
9331'

Maggie
Lakes

Alpine

Trout

MOUNTAIN

MAGGIE
MOUNTAIN
GROVE

Maggie
Mountain
10,042'

HOME

296

Creek

MOUNTAIN

SILVER
CREEK
GROVE

Creek

Mountaineer

Wilderness

HOME

the Burro

BURRO
CREEK
GROVE

Creek

Kern

Creek

River

STATE

GROVE

WISHON
GROVE

Bear

220

of

North

Alder

Creek

North

Creek

Creek

FOREST

Creek

South

Fork

Fish

Fork

ALDER CREEK
GROVE

Alder

Creek

NATIONAL

Clicks

208

North

Sequoia Crest

Jordan Peak
9115'

216

iddle Fork

McIntyre

Creek

190

South

Tule River

FREEMAN
CREEK
GROVE

190

Fork

Camp Nelson

MCINTYRE

22S82

of

GROVE

Creek

21S50

Deadman's Creek

the

Bateman Ridge

BLACK

21S94

21S12

MOUNTAIN

Solo Peak
7310'

GROVE

Ponderosa

FOREST

TULE

22S8

21S94

RIVER

Slate Mountain
9302'

RED HILL
GROVE

Creek

LEGEND

INDIAN

RESERVATION

Windy

Creek

PEYRONE
GROVE

River

Tule

SOUTH
PEYRONE
GROVE

Fork

Cedar

Creek

21S94

Onion Meadow
Peak
8306'

South

HIGHWAY

DIVIDE

WESTERN

Main Road

Paved Road

Unpaved Road

Trail

Sequoia Groves

National Park

National Forest

State Forest

Indian Land

0   .5   1   1.5   2   2.5 Miles

0   1   2   3   4 Kilom

22S82

CALIFORNIA

GROVES IN THE TULE RIVER WATERSHED

MOUNTAIN HOME GROVE   89

MAGGIE MOUNTAIN, SILVER CREEK,   94
BURRO CREEK, AND WISHON GROVES

ALDER CREEK GROVE   95

MCINTYRE GROVE   96

BLACK MOUNTAIN GROVE   97

RED HILL GROVE   100

PEYRONE GROVE   100

SOUTH PEYRONE GROVE   101

PARKER PEAK AND NORTH COLD   101
SPRING GROVES

MOUNTAIN HOME GROVE

Size: Large
Type: Mixed
Manager: Mountain Home State Forest (most), Tulare County
(Balch County Park), and Sequoia National Forest
Access: Paved road

Mountain Home Grove is one of the largest and most impressive groves, despite the past logging of many of its old growth sequoias. John Muir was probably referring to the grove when he said that the North Fork of the Tule River watershed had "the finest block of the Big Tree forest in the entire belt." Exceptionally large trees are found at this ideal sequoia growing site, where the species thrives over a broad landscape, not just in inner drainages and moist pockets.

Pond in Mountain Home Grove.

The grove is centered in plateau-like terrain in the headwaters of Rancheria and Bear Creeks. From the plateau, the grove also spreads downslope to the east. A narrow grove section in Moses Gulch connects the plateau and upper-slope grove areas with another major grove section in the canyon of the North Fork of the Middle Fork (also known as the Wishon Fork) of the Tule River.

In the canyon, the grove forms a relatively unbroken belt from Galena Creek on the south to about the 7,200 foot level in the Golden Trout Wilderness (about a mile north of Redwood Crossing). In some locations, the canyon sequoias impressively ascend the slopes, reaching their greatest width in the Redwood Crossing area. The canyon grove is primarily confined to riverside terrain in its northern reaches. One striking outlier group consists of eight mature sequoias (and several younger trees) growing at 7,800 feet on the upper east-facing slopes of Moses Mountain, isolated on both sides by avalanche chutes. While the canyon section has been separately identified as the "Moses Mountain" or "Middle Tule" grove by some, the plateau and canyon sections of Mountain Home Grove are better considered to be a single grove, as they are contiguous.

The largest portion of Mountain Home Grove is managed as part of Mountain Home State Forest. Some of the fringe areas of the grove's plateau section and much of the canyon section are managed by Sequoia National Forest. A few small parcels near Rancheria Creek on the west edge of the grove, with very few mature sequoias, are still private and include residential development.

In contrast to the grove's managed plateau section, much of the grove's canyon section (the part north of the Hidden Falls River Road crossing) is unlogged wilderness. The northernmost extension of the canyon sequoias has been included in the Golden Trout Wilderness, and thus legislatively protected. Other pristine sections of the canyon section have been safeguarded by administrative policy, but they lack assured legislative protection. Part of the grove is also shielded from destructive logging because it is included in Balch Park, operated by Tulare County.

The Methuselah Tree in Mountain Home Grove.

Early photo of Methuselah Tree.

From the foothills, a seasonal paved loop route (known as Bear Creek Road on the south and as Balch Park Road on the north) ascends steeply to the grove plateau and circles through the grove. Road access is usually reliable only until the first heavy snow. East of the main loop road, the well-maintained dirt Summit Road curves through the eastern part of the Mountain Home plateau. Summit Road is a spectacular drive—an almost non-stop "avenue of the giants." From it, short dirt spur roads access sights such as the Methuselah Tree and an extremely fine concentration of giants east of Dogwood Meadow, including the Genesis Tree. The River Road, also dirt, descends to the canyon section of the grove and the river. It crosses the river (only in low water conditions) and continues south on the east side to near Silver Creek Grove.

There are numerous trails and closed dirt roads suitable for hiking on the plateau. The trail through unlogged Moses Gulch links the plateau and canyon sections of the grove. Remarkably scenic trails reach the wilderness canyon of the upper river, commencing from trailheads at Shake Camp and the river crossing. The grove has several car campgrounds (including large Frasier Mill and Balch Park Campgrounds) and walk-in camps near the river.

There have never been reliable sequoia inventories of the full grove. Mountain Home State Forest officials estimate that its portion of the grove includes about 4,000 sequoias 5 feet in diameter (at breast height) or larger. It probably has well over 1,000 specimens over 10 feet. Balch Park has an estimated 200 adult sequoias.

GROVES IN THE TULE RIVER WATERSHED

Dogwood Meadow, Mountain Home Grove.

Mountain Home Grove.

The mature sequoias in the national forest sections of the grove have not been counted, but probably number well over 100. Most of the old growth is in the plateau section, but the uninventoried canyon section, where sequoias were never logged, has several hundred mature giants.

Generally, the canyon section of the grove has relatively smaller sequoias, which dominate the forest in impressive densities in several areas. At one unnamed trailside location just southeast of Redwood Crossing, forty or more sequoias are visible from one spot.

Most of the sequoia logging that occurred until 1945 was selective; old growth sequoias survive in most of the logged grove areas. The grove has abundant post-logging sequoia growth, including stands aged 100 years or more (see the Frasier Mill Campground, for example). Younger sequoias date from the time logging ended in the 1940s and later. Some of the naturally regenerated young stands are composed of up to 95 percent sequoia, rather than the a more common mix of conifer types.

The non-sequoia forest outside the wilderness canyon section is generally young and mid-aged mixed conifers, except for isolated small areas of old growth such as along the Moses Gulch trail corridor. There is an isolated 100 acres of red fir near the former Camp Lena site.

The plateau section of the grove is one of the most impressive sites in the Sierra for exceptionally large sequoias. Wendell Flint found that Mountain Home Grove was home to more of the 40 known surviving sequoias with total volumes of over 30,000 cubic feet than any grove except Giant Forest. It is also a leading site for research on young sequoia growth under differing conditions.

The broken-topped Methuselah Tree and the Adam Tree (once regarded as the grove's largest) were long recognized for their size. But others in the Mountain Home Grove, such as the Summit and Euclid Trees, received little attention until recently. The Genesis Tree, just east of (above) Dogwood Meadow in an area filled with exceptionally large specimens, was not identified as the grove's largest specimen until 1985. It contends with the Boole and the Stagg Trees for the distinction of being the sixth largest tree.

Mountain Home Grove endured several stages of old growth sequoia logging. Many mills logged sequoias in the grove between 1870 and 1905. These early mill operations were usually unprofitable, very limited in geographic scale, and short-lived. Following a period of about thirty-five years without significant logging in the grove, the Rouch and Hedrick mills logged there intensively from 1941 to 1945, generating the public controversy that resulted in state acquisition of almost all of the private land in the grove. In 1956, a final upsetting episode of selective sequoia logging occurred on a since-acquired private inholding.

Most of the earliest logging (primarily of pine) in the Rancheria Creek area was conducted on public land, before regulations had been issued and before permits or surveys were required. In 1884, the grove experienced a "land rush," and by the 1890s most of the area was in private ownership. By 1885, intensive logging for sequoia and other timber was underway, and such logging was

View east to Maggie Mountain from Mountain Home Grove.

Dogwood Meadow at Mountain Home Grove.

continued by a series of mills until 1905. Timber was generally chuted to the mills, and then transported by flume or hauled to the Central Valley below.

Some of the largest and oldest grove specimens were logged in the early era. These trees grew near what became the Enterprise Mill site, in an area now close to one of the main grove roads. The Centennial Tree, reputed to be the largest tree in the grove, was felled in the mid-1870s. Through tree ring analysis, its age has been set at 3,117 years. Another nearby logged giant also exceeded 3,000 years. The short-lived Enterprise Mill nearly clearcut its vicinity, in the grove's most intensive early logging episode. In a limited tree-ring study of only fifty stumps in 1911-12 in the Enterprise Mill site area, Ellsworth Huntington identified fifteen specimens that had exceeded 2,000 years of age.

The logging between 1941 and 1945 affected many areas in the southern grove, east of Balch Park, and near Shake Camp that had escaped early logging. Much of this logging has been characterized as "intensified spite-cutting" designed to force a government purchase at a higher price.

In the 1940s sequoias were typically felled by blasting rather than cutting, leaving shattered stumps when blasting was done above ground, and uprooted stumps when smaller sequoias were blasted from below ground.

The mills at this time were not large, but they did not need to be because the market was for unmilled, split post and shake sequoia products. Logging was intensive, and in the five years up to 1945, the total timber harvested was equal to the amount cut in about thirty years during the early logging era. One state investigator concluded that this cutting included nearly 300 mature sequoias. Incomplete information indicates that most of the sequoia cutting was of relatively small sequoias (under ten feet in diameter). A local newspaper reported that one logged sequoia was twenty-six feet in diameter.

Since public acquisition in 1946, the state forest management of its section of Mountain Home Grove has differed from that of both the park service and forest service. While the objective has been a relatively light level of timber production, large sequoias have been strictly protected and scenic qualities have been preserved by exclusive, careful use of selective logging techniques. Though sequoias are favored, management activities have preserved mixed-conifer diversity. There also has been an attempt to preserve sugar pine within the state forest, despite the white pine blister rust epidemic affecting that species.

MAGGIE MOUNTAIN, SILVER CREEK, BURRO CREEK, AND WISHON GROVES

Size: Burro Creek: Mid-size; all others: Small
Type: Wilderness old growth
Manager: Maggie Mountain, Burro Creek, and Wishon: Sequoia National Forest; Silver Creek: Mountain Home State Forest (most) and Sequoia National Forest.
Access: Maggie Mountain and Burro Creek: Cross-country; Silver Creek and Wishon: Trail

East of the upper North Fork of the Middle Fork of the Tule River, across the canyon from the Mountain Home Grove plateau, are remote and little-visited Maggie Mountain, Silver Creek, Burro Creek, and Wishon Groves (listed north to south). Each is in a wilderness condition, with never-logged, sequoia forest. Most exploration of these groves requires cross-country travel; only Silver Creek and Wishon Groves have any trail access.

The small Maggie Mountain Grove is located in the headwaters of Galena Creek. It features a small but vigorous forest of primarily younger sequoias growing picturesquely at an elevation above 7,500 feet, in close proximity to steep, granite slopes above. Other grove sequoias are narrowly scattered along the creek for a considerable distance below. A trail crosses Galena Creek between the two units of relatively small mature sequoias.

Silver Creek Grove is thinly distributed along Silver Creek at elevations between 5,100 and 6,200 feet. The grove is about 100 acres in size. A trail crosses its lower edge, near the river, and another crosses Silver Creek at elevations above the grove. In between, nearly the entire grove is trail-less. The grove probably has more than one hundred mature sequoias of relatively small sizes.

Burro Creek Grove is the largest of the four groves, with about 300 acres spread over more than 1,500 feet of elevation range.

Located primarily along the North Fork of Burro Creek, the grove is trail-less, and almost all of it is on steep, densely-forested, constantly challenging terrain. It contains more than one hundred mature sequoias, including several scattered, difficult-to-find immense individuals.

Wishon Grove extends for about one mile in a slim band along the North Fork of the Middle Fork of the Tule River, south of Mountain Home Grove and Burro Creek. It has one of the lowest elevations of any grove, from about 4,400 to 4,750 feet. A trail passes through the best part of the grove on the east side of the river.

ALDER CREEK GROVE

Size: Mid-size
Type: Old growth
Manager: Private owners and Sequoia National Forest
Access: Paved road

Mid-sized Alder Creek is the only sequoia grove that is home to a substantially developed private residential subdivision, Sequoia Crest. The subdivision was developed in the 1950s in a prime section of the grove, after the site's pines and firs were logged. Fortunately, almost all of the large sequoias were preserved.

The grove is easily accessible over about six miles of paved road north from Highway 190 near Camp Nelson; loop drives wind throughout the subdivision. Homes have been erected amidst the abundant old growth sequoias, and the image of timeless giants beside modern vacation houses is unsettling. The strange visual impact of the development shouldn't distract visitors from the recognition that the grove is a fine sequoia site. One hundred and fifty or more mature sequoias survive, including many very large specimens.

Part of the private land north of the developed area is still largely natural, on slopes above the South Fork of Alder Creek, and accessible from a dead-end dirt road. Here grows the Stagg Tree. It is perhaps the sixth largest sequoia in total volume and boasts a ground perimeter of 109 feet that is second only to that of the Boole Tree among the largest volume sequoias. At 60 feet above ground, it is still about 18.2 feet in diameter, and thicker than the General Sherman Tree. The nearby Day Tree has a freakishly large base buttress, giving it the largest known base perimeter (155 feet) of any known sequoia, though it is not exceptionally large for a sequoia overall.

When seen from viewpoints a short cross-country jaunt to the north, the strip of forest surrounding the Stagg Tree on the south side of the South Fork of Alder Creek is an inspiring spectacle of shaggy-topped "giant forest" that looks as wild as any, despite its proximity to the developed grove section. From vantage points north of the creek, the development is out of sight, and the strikingly fine original quality of this forest is apparent. Unfortunately, the grove's values were not recognized by conservationists early enough to keep the grove a natural preserve.

A major section of the grove is on undeveloped Sequoia National

Alder Creek Grove with residential development!

Forest land on trail-less, lower elevation slopes northwest of the private development. In addition to mammoth old growth specimens, the grove has abundant smaller giants.

MCINTYRE GROVE

Size: Large
Type: Old growth, partly wilderness
Manager: Sequoia National Forest
Access: Paved road

McIntyre Grove.

McIntyre Grove is one of the magnificent large, riverside groves in Sequoia National Forest. Its dense sequoias flank both sides of the Middle Fork of the Tule River for miles, and climb the canyon slopes, particularly south of the river. Some logging has occurred, primarily for non-sequoia conifers, but nearly all of the old growth sequoias survive. Much of the grove is wilderness.

To the west of the sizable main grove, a small second unit (sometimes called the "Carr Wilson Grove") occurs in a stringer configuration along Bear Creek.

The grove is easily reached by road from all-season Highway 190, just east of the mountain settlement of Camp Nelson. Belknap Campground is in the west end of the grove. Higher elevation viewpoints on Highway 190 offer distant panoramic grove vistas, particularly of the upper grove.

McIntyre Grove has excellent trails. A superbly scenic sequoia trail along the river through the heart of the grove ascends from the campground to a trailhead on Highway 190 (about a half-mile west of Quaking Aspen campground). Steep Bear Creek Trail climbs from the Coy Flat Road to the crest of Slate Mountain ridge at over 9,000 feet, passing a dense, high-elevation stand of some of the grove's largest sequoias, including the Patriarch Tree. That specimen, one of the Sierra's notable sequoias, is relatively short, and does not have a large base, but its trunk is massive and has almost no taper. It is believed to be one of the oldest living sequoias.

The grove probably has more than 2,000 mature sequoias, though a full sequoia inventory is lacking. Giants over 10 feet in diameter (at breast height) are abundant, but the grove is not known for exceptionally large specimens. This is probably due to the frequent intense fires over the centuries in the grove's canyon terrain. These fires have also created a paucity of large sequoia snags; such snags are common in less fire-vulnerable groves like Giant Forest.

Most of the grove is never-logged forest, particularly the eastern and higher elevation sections. Significant whitewood logging occurred on both sides of the river in the central and western parts of the grove from the 1920s to the 1950s, but the cutting was limited enough that the forest has recovered a natural appearance.

The grove has not had any major twentieth-century fire (primarily because of the fire suppression policy), and unnaturally heavy woody fuel has built up. The grove is vulnerable to an intense wildfire that could, at worst, sweep dangerously through the whole canyon. No doubt such devastating fires occurred before settlement, and recent human management of the landscape doesn't assure that it won't happen again.

Almost all the grove south of the river is habitat for the spotted owl. Because that grove section is contiguous to long-protected sections of the Slate Mountain Roadless area, this splendid grove is, fortunately, part of a larger block of protected forest lands. It was not just a small "island" of protected old growth as many forest service groves were before creation of the new Giant Sequoia National Monument.

BLACK MOUNTAIN GROVE

Size: Large
Type: Mixed
Manager: Sequoia National Forest (most), Tule River Indian Reservation, private owners
Access: Dirt road

Black Mountain Grove is one of the largest groves in area (with more than 2,000 acres), and it ranks no lower than sixth among all groves in total number of large sequoias. Few groves have more exceptionally large specimens. Surprisingly, Black Mountain is one of the least known and least visited of the major groves. A visitor can expect to car tour or hike among the grove giants with almost complete privacy (outside of deer hunting season).

The grove sprawls majestically over both sides of the divide between the South Fork of the Middle Fork and the South Fork of the Tule River. (The divide roughly coincides with the boundary between the Tule River Indian Reservation and Sequoia National Forest.) Most of the grove is in Sequoia National Forest, and prime grove areas there are accessible by good quality dirt roads and short, rugged, cross-country hikes. Parts of the grove are on the Indian reservation and on a few private parcels with restricted public access.

A winding, low-speed auto tour of more than nine miles through the giants, with some panoramic vistas, can be made on the primary east-west dirt road through the grove (Road 21S12). This is the longest single driveable road in any grove. There are no recreational facilities or maintained trails.

Relatively few sequoias were logged at Black Mountain, leaving over 2,300 surviving mature sequoias, far more than in most groves. The trees are exceptionally large; a 1935 survey of less than half of the grove identified 147 sequoias reaching 15 feet or larger in diameter (at 6 feet above mean ground level). Other inventories have indicated that, proportionately, the grove's mature sequoias are older than the mature sequoia populations of most other groves.

Fire-scarred giant in Black Mountain Grove.

The Black Mountain Beauty, the grove's largest known sequoia, is located in an area clearcut of its whitewood in the 1980s. Wendell Flint measured it to have a total volume greater than more famous trees such as the largest in the Calaveras Groves and the Bull Buck

The sequoia is the world's largest tree in total size (as measured by volume), though it is not the thickest or tallest tree species. There have been thicker African baobab trees and one thicker tule cypress in Mexico. Australian eucalyptus trees and coast redwoods commonly grow taller.

Sequoias are also the world's largest living things except for three organisms that spread over acres and are visually unrecognizable as single living beings. These are groves of clonally identical aspen and the underground fungus types *Armillaria bulbosa* and *Armillaria ostoyae*.

Sequoia scholar Wendell Flint has documented the measurements of the largest twenty or so known specimens. The General Sherman Tree is far and away the biggest in total size. Its total trunk volume was calculated to be about 52,508 cubic feet, which is almost 10 percent greater than its nearest competitor, the Washington Tree of Giant Forest. When measured, the Sherman was about 275 feet tall, with a ground perimeter of 102.6 feet. It was 25.1 feet in diameter (at breast height) and an impressive 17.3 feet in diameter at 120 feet above the ground.

The tallest sequoia is unknown. The tallest specimens have not attracted the attention that those of largest diameter have. On uneven terrain in thick forest, it is more difficult to identify and measure tall specimens. There is a relative paucity of reliable sequoia height measurements, compared with more abundant and reliable diameter measurements. Several sequoias have been reported to be in the 305 to 315 foot height range. The higher figure is probably close to the maximum sequoia height. But considering that thousands of tall specimens have not had height measurements, it is probable that the tallest specimen is yet to be identified. Typically, large old growth sequoias are in the range of 240 to 275 feet tall, usually with some top-shortening damage or dieback.

General Sherman Tree.

Clearcuts surround the Three Sisters in Black Mountain Grove, 1986.

Black Mountain Beauty.

of Nelder Grove. Another specimen has a larger base than the Beauty, but lesser overall size due to a broken top. The Beauty may not even be the grove's largest, as many huge sequoias here have yet to be measured.

Despite instances of logging dating from before 1900, the grove has retained impressive small areas of mature, old growth forest with abundant sequoias. Relatively undisturbed stands are below Road 21S12 in the drainages of the West Fork of Wilson Creek and of Deadman Creek, in sections of the steep upper north slopes of Solo Peak, and on the divide east of Solo Peak. These are all roadless and trail-less areas. Grove areas logged in the 1950s or earlier often have excellent stands of second growth sequoia. Much of the grove's non-sequoia forest is made up of relatively young mixed conifers due to a major 1926 fire, as well as to extensive logging.

A large block of pristine grove forest, perhaps 500 acres or more in the drainages of the West Fork of Wilson Creek and Deadman Creek, suffered heavy logging in the 1980s, including seven white-wood clearcuts. In these clearcuts, large sequoias weren't logged, but almost all of the mature pine and fir were cut in affected areas. Conservationist protests and legal challenges came too late to stop this destruction, though public outcry against this forest service logging subsequently led the agency to abandon its 1988 plans to log 900 acres of the grove. These clearcuts have created a bizarre mix of surviving giants and very young conifers, without intermediate-aged mixed conifers. Several of the cut over areas can be easily viewed from primary dirt roads through the grove.

The grove is well-watered by the perennial and intermittent headwaters of several creeks, including Wilson, Deadman, and Long Canyon Creek tributaries to the Middle Fork of the Tule River, in the national forest part of the grove.

The Mountain Aire private residential subdivision at the east end of the grove is one of only two such developments in groves (see Alder Creek Grove above). Mountain Aire has no utility service or winter access, and most of its lots have not been developed as of 1999.

One of the unusual fine old growth sugar pine stands remaining in the southern Sierra is just west of the grove, on the trail-less north side of Black Mountain Ridge.

RED HILL GROVE

Size: Mid-size
Type: Old growth
Manager: Sequoia National Forest (most), Tule River Indian
Reservation, and private owners
Access: Dirt and paved road

Mid-sized Red Hill Grove is "off-the-beaten track," but still easy to
reach by road. From the north, the approach (which first passes
through Black Mountain Grove) provides a scenic overview of the
grove, before winding down through it. Red Hill Grove, in the well-
watered headwaters of the South Fork of the Tule River, is one of
three groves (along with Peyrone and South Peyrone) on Sequoia
National Forest land at higher elevations east of the Tule River
Indian Reservation. Many of the finest trees are in the main South
Fork drainage, west of the access road. A bit of the grove extends
into the Indian reservation, and the road passes through one private
inholding where sequoias have been protected, but which was selectively logged for whitewoods.

The grove typifies the several Sequoia National Forest sequoia
groves that have never been publicized or significantly used for
recreation. Despite the grove's attractions, there are no trails or
interpretive signs.

The Red Hill sequoias haven't been logged to any significant
extent. They total perhaps 500 or more mature trees, scattered over
several hundred acres. Though large specimens are common, none
are known to be of exceptional size. Selective logging of pine and fir
has been done, but the forest service part of the grove retains significant old growth mixed-conifer stands. Fortunately, many of the big
pines and fir of Red Hill Grove survive, in contrast to other Sequoia
National Forest groves where whitewood clearcut logging took
place in the 1980s.

PEYRONE GROVE

Size: Mid-size
Type: Old growth
Manager: Sequoia National Forest and Tule River Indian
Reservation
Access: Trail (closed dirt road)

Peyrone Grove is a mid-sized Sequoia National Forest grove in two
units, with many scattered outlying sequoias, in the Windy Creek
drainage south of Red Hill Grove. A small part of the grove extends
west into the Tule River Indian Reservation. Unlike Red Hill Grove,
Peyrone cannot be seen from nearby roadside vista points. With
binoculars and a trained eye, however, one can observe in distant
northern panoramas how widely the Peyrone Grove's sequoias
extend. The forest service has reported that the grove has more than
400 "museum type" sequoias, as well as numerous younger specimens. The largest trees haven't been authoritatively inventoried.

Peyrone Grove giants after 1980s logging.

Until the Crawford Road (which extends from Black Mountain Grove through Red Hill Grove to the east, and southeast to the Western Divide Highway) was built in the 1980s, Peyrone Grove was remote wilderness with dense old growth forest. The new spur road to the grove's northern unit made possible heavy logging of pine and fir in the late 1980s. Now old growth sequoias stand out starkly in some large whitewood clearcuts. Other sections of the grove retain their old growth character. Closed logging roads developed in the 1980s serve as trail access.

SOUTH PEYRONE GROVE

Size: Small
Type: Wilderness old growth
Manager: Sequoia National Forest
Access: Cross-country

South Peyrone Grove, an unheralded, small, and densely packed pocket of forty or more mature sequoias, was not commonly recognized as a separate grove until 1992. It is in old growth, wilderness condition in the Cedar Creek drainage, about a mile south of Peyrone Grove. Access requires challenging cross-country travel.

PARKER PEAK AND NORTH COLD SPRING GROVES

Size: Parker Peak: Mid-size; North Cold Spring: Small
Type: Old growth
Manager: Tule River Indian Reservation
Access: Restricted (inquire for current policies)

Mid-sized Parker Peak Grove and neighboring North Cold Spring Grove, about a mile to the west, are the only two groves entirely within the Tule River Indian Reservation. Current reservation policy does not allow unrestricted public access. Inquire for current access requirements.

Parker Peak Grove has more than 100 mature sequoias and North Cold Spring Grove probably has somewhat over 25 large specimens. The old growth sequoias escaped logging in both groves. Reservation practice has been to protect the old growth sequoias, while selectively harvesting other timber and naturally fallen sequoias.

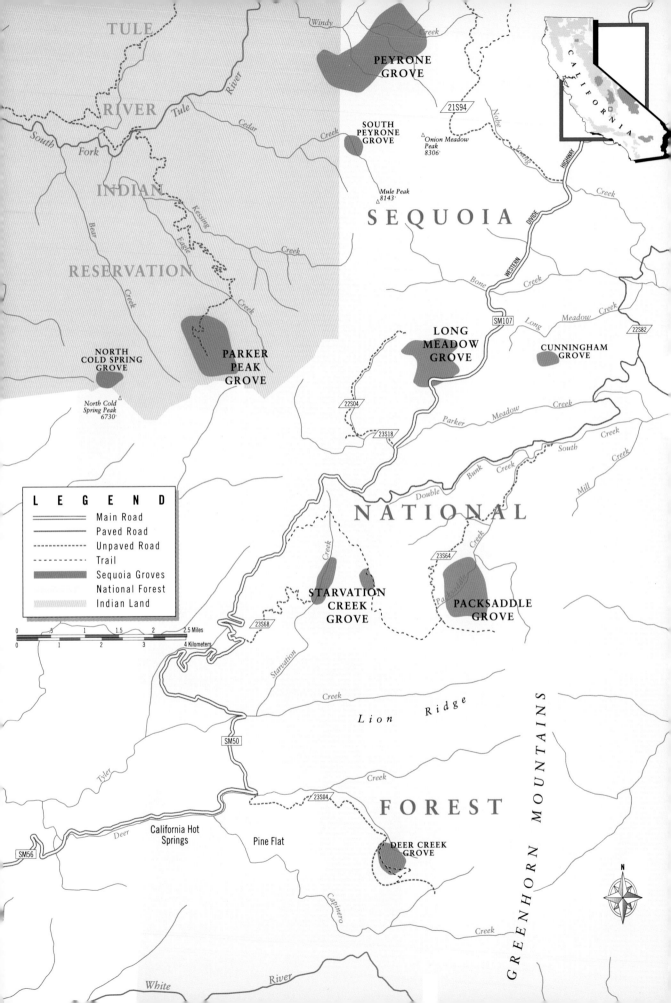

OTHER SOUTHERN SIERRA GROVES

FREEMAN CREEK GROVE   105

LONG MEADOW AND CUNNINGHAM   106
GROVES

PACKSADDLE GROVE   108

STARVATION CREEK GROVE   109

DEER CREEK GROVE   109

FREEMAN CREEK GROVE

Size: Large
Type: Old growth
Manager: Sequoia National Forest
Access: Paved and dirt road

Freeman Creek Grove in Sequoia National Forest is usually considered to be the finest of all the national forest groves. With an area well over 1,500 acres, this is the largest unlogged grove outside of a national park. It is also the easternmost grove. Picturesquely filling most of the basin of Freeman Creek in the Kern River watershed, it is one of four groves there that, while still west of the Sierra crest, are not on the Sierra's primary west slope (where all other groves are located). Because of its exceptional site in a largely unspoiled basin, the grove has been protected as part of a larger botanic area covering most of the watershed of Freeman Creek.

View north from the Needles to the High Sierra over lower Freeman Creek.

There is road access to trailheads at the top (west) and bottom (east) ends of the grove, but the heart of the grove is roadless, wild, and undeveloped except for one maintained trail. There are also some unofficial, unmaintained, short trails in the lower grove that lead to a few of the largest sequoia specimens. Most of the grove, however, is trail-less, including much of the area of dense old giants south of Freeman Creek.

The old growth sequoias survive in majestic abundance, including many very large specimens. Partial sequoia inventories indicate that the grove may have more than 2,000 sequoias at least 5 feet in diameter (at breast height), and more than 800 over 10 feet in diameter. Probably more than 100 grove sequoias have diameters that exceed 15 feet. The recently publicized, off-trail Goshawk Tree is probably the largest grove sequoia, with a volume of over 32,000 cubic feet. Nearby is the fire-hollowed, broken-off Telescope Tree (also known as the Castro Tree), which is also over 20 feet in diameter.

The grove's non-sequoia vegetation is more varied than in many groves. Red fir is the primary sequoia conifer associate in the relatively cool environment of the highest grove elevations on the west. At about 5,500 feet on the east, conditions are far more hot and dry than one would expect for old growth areas, and sequoias are found near sagebrush, which usually grows in dry, desert-like conditions. Ample subsurface water is obviously available, however, because some of the largest sequoias in the grove grow at these lower elevations. Most of the grove has virgin mixed-conifer forest, full of large sugar and Jeffrey pines and white fir.

As recently as 1986, the U.S. Forest Service planned new roads and heavy logging of mature whitewoods within the grove. Fortunately, conservationist challenges to ongoing logging in other groves led the agency to abandon its Freeman Creek logging plans.

While new logging would have destroyed the wilderness quality of the grove, Freeman Creek Grove is one place where limited and careful cutting might actually contribute to sequoia preservation. Much of the grove has an unnaturally dense growth of understory white fir and heavy accumulations of woody debris due to fire suppression. It is a high risk location for intense, old-growth-sequoia-destroying wildfire. In-depth site studies are needed before detailed fuel reduction proposals can be presented for public review and then implemented.

The Needles Trail on the high divide south of the grove has fabulous views of Mount Whitney, the Golden Trout Wilderness, the Freeman and Lloyd Meadow Creeks basin, and old growth conifers along the trail.

LONG MEADOW AND CUNNINGHAM GROVES

Size: Long Meadow: Mid-size; Cunningham: Tiny
Type: Old growth
Manager: Sequoia National Forest
Access: Long Meadow: Paved road; Cunningham: Trail (closed road)

Long Meadow and Cunningham Groves are among the four groves that grow in the Kern River watershed, east of the primary west slope of the Sierra. Mid-sized Long Meadow is one of the best known and most visited because the Western Divide Highway passes through it. It is a fine aggregation of large old growth specimens. The Sequoia National Forest interpretive Trail of 100 Giants winds through the lower grove, and Redwood Meadow Campground is nearby.

Long Meadow Grove was never logged for sequoias, and it probably has more than 200 giants at least 10 feet in diameter (at breast height), as well as numerous smaller specimens. Though it lacks enormous specimens, it is one of the groves where the mature sequoias tend to be older and larger.

Most of the grove is on the east side of Table Mountain Ridge, extending from the highway to near the ridge top. A smaller, separate unit is on the west side of the ridge. The forest is primarily fine old growth, mixed-conifer east of the ridge, a small emerald island in an overlogged landscape beyond the narrow greenbelt flanking the highway.

The entire west unit of Long Meadow Grove was clearcut for whitewoods in the 1980s. That cut is obvious from the western approach route, is very large in area, is practically devoid of other conifers, and has a high density of surviving large sequoias. Some whitewoods also were harvested in the 1980s in the main Long Meadow unit, and at least fifteen large, previously-fallen sequoias were harvested in another regrettable change to the grove's character.

Cunningham is among the smallest of all the Sierra groves. It is a pocket of a few acres about one mile northeast of Long Meadow Grove. Its old growth sequoias survive, but there are only about fifteen large specimens. Cunningham Grove is another tiny "island" of old growth in the generally overlogged "Western Divide" section of Sequoia National Forest. It is puzzling that sequoias survived in

This old sequoia in Long Meadow Grove fell in April 1997 after surrounding trees were logged in the 1980s.

OTHER SOUTHERN SIERRA GROVES

Some fear that natural sequoia groves are shrinking due to their limited distribution and twentieth-century climatic warming trends. Others assert that the sequoia resource is "just hanging on," and that the natural groves could disappear in a millennium or less. Studies suggest otherwise. Only minor changes in grove sizes have been detected in recent centuries. Most groves are maintaining or even slightly expanding their size. Despite alarmist fears of inadequate sequoia regrowth, sequoias can and frequently do vigorously regenerate in grove areas with adequate soil and light conditions. So far, there has been no demonstrated effect of climate change on sequoia regeneration and growth in suitable sites.

Recent research indicates that the sequoia population is now as high as it has been for the past several centuries. While logging did substantially reduce the population of mature sequoias, most of the mature and old growth sequoias survived. The number of literally "giant" sequoias over eight feet in diameter will continue to increase in the absence of logging, wildfire, and other catastrophic events. From a global perspective, the sequoia resource is unusual in that it is improving in quality, rather than diminishing like so many other prized species.

Cunningham Grove's isolated location while they are not found in many areas with comparable growing conditions.

A dirt logging road nearly reaches the grove, but the grove must be explored cross-country. An unnaturally overgrown understory due to past fire suppression has created a high, localized fire hazard. The grove's small size allows the forest service to reduce the fuel hazard by controlled burning or other techniques which are not destructive to the old growth resources.

PACKSADDLE GROVE

Size: Mid-size
Type: Old growth
Manager: Sequoia National Forest
Access: Dirt road

Packsaddle is a very fine, mid-sized grove. It is another instance of old growth pines, firs, and sequoias being surrounded by Sequoia National Forest land long managed for timber production. Though little visited, it is one of the nicest forests of its size in the Sierra Nevada. Packsaddle is also one of the few Sequoia National Forest groves that has retained its old growth character despite the fact that it lacked any official protective designation for most of the twentieth century. The new Giant Sequoia National Monument protects it from commercial logging. This also assures that it will continue to be recognized as a prime spotted owl habitat area.

The grove has more than 100 giants over 10 feet in diameter (at breast height) and abundant smaller specimens, in a widely scattered distribution. Perhaps 5 or 6 specimens are over 20 feet in diameter. For its size, Packsaddle Grove has a notable number of exceptionally large specimens. The Packsaddle Giant has the fourth largest known ground perimeter (106.3 feet), and the nearby General Lee Tree (also known as the Ghost Tree) could have been among the Sierra's largest specimens before it lost its top long ago. Some of the grove's biggest specimens are near its south edge, a short hike from the dirt road on the grove's south edge.

Because the grove is just a bit over a mile east from the Starvation Creek Grove site, where the last active California condor nest in the Sierra Nevada was found in 1984, it is recognized as one of the locations for potential future use by condors, if and when they are reintroduced into the area.

The grove edge can easily be reached by dirt road, but the grove interior is trail-less and suitable for exploration only by strong cross-country hikers comfortable in rugged, dense forest.

Packsaddle Giant.

STARVATION CREEK GROVE

Size: Small
Type: Old growth
Manager: Sequoia National Forest
Access: Trail (closed dirt road)

Sequoia National Forest's Starvation Creek Grove has two small units, a narrow stringer of giants along Starvation Creek and a separate unit just below a logging road about three tenths mile east of the upper edge of the creekside unit.

The east section was the site of the last active California condor nest in the wild (before condors were reintroduced to the wild of the California coast ranges in 1992.) In February 1984, an adult pair and a chick were discovered during whitewood logging operations in the grove. The condors were captured and removed to a zoo, as part of the U.S. Fish and Wildlife Service's condor recovery captive breeding program. The cavity that was the condor's nest location can be seen high up the trunk of the snag-top Condor Nest Tree, which adjoins a whitewood clearcut. It is not yet certain if and when condors will be released into the wild again in the Sierra Nevada. Should that occur, the grove may become a nest site again.

Starvation Creek Grove.

The grove units preserve tiny patches of old growth, including old growth mixed conifers, in a vicinity that has been heavily logged over the years. Perhaps 20 to 30 mature sequoias survive in the creekside unit and about 20 to 25 in the east unit. None is exceptionally large. One can hike on closed dirt logging roads to the edge of both grove units, but there are no trails within the grove.

DEER CREEK GROVE

Size: Small
Type: Old growth
Manager: Sequoia National Forest
Access: Dirt road

Small Deer Creek Grove is the most southern grove, about 250 air miles south of northernmost Placer County Grove. It has about 35 mature sequoias strung along the creek, plus many younger trees. None is exceptionally large. The lower edge of the grove is accessible by good dirt road, and a trail passes by all the grove's good-sized trees. The grove was selectively logged for pine and fir only between 1914 and 1920, but it has been preserved from cutting since then. The grove's protection within the new Giant Sequoia National Monument means that it will remain fine spotted owl habitat.

Deer Creek Grove.

USGS TOPOGRAPHICAL MAPS WITH GIANT SEQUOIA GROVES

The sequoia groves are listed alphabetically below, followed by names of the United States Geological Survey (USGS) 7.5 minute topographical map(s) that cover the grove area.

Grove	USGS Topographic Maps
Wren Peak	
Alder Creek	Camp Wishon, Camp Nelson
Atwell-East Fork	Silver City
Bearskin	General Grant Grove
Big Stump	General Grant Grove
Black Mountain	Solo Peak, Camp Nelson
Board Camp	Moses Mountain
Boulder Creek	Wren Peak
Burro Creek	Camp Wishon
Cahoon Creek	Silver City
Case Mountain	Case Mountain
Castle Creek	Lodgepole
Cherry Gap	Hume
Coffeepot Canyon	Silver City
Converse Basin	Hume, Verplank Ridge
Cunningham	Johnsondale
Deer Creek	Tobias Peak
Deer Meadow	Wren Peak
Dennison	Dennison Peak
Devils Canyon	Dennison Peak
Eden Creek	Silver City
Evans	Wren Peak
Freeman Creek	Camp Nelson, Hockett Peak, Sentinel Peak
Garfield-Dillonwood	Moses Mountain
Giant Forest	Giant Forest, Lodgepole
Grant	General Grant Grove, Hume
Homers Nose	Moses Mountain, Silver City
Horse Creek	Silver City
Indian Basin	Hume
Kennedy	Wren Peak
Landslide	Hume, Muir Grove
Little Boulder Creek	Wren Peak, Muir Grove
Lockwood	Wren Peak
Long Meadow	Johnsondale
Lost	Muir Grove

Grove	USGS Topographic Maps
Maggie Mountain	Moses Mountain
Mariposa	Mariposa Grove
McIntyre	Camp Nelson, Sentinel Peak
McKinley	Nelson Mountain
Merced	El Portal (the grove), Lake Eleanor (the vicinity)
Monarch	Wren Peak
Mountain Home	Moses Mountain, Camp Wishon
Muir	Muir Grove
Nelder	White Chief Mountain
New Oriole	Silver City
North Cold Spring	California Hot Springs
North Calaveras	Dorrington
Oriole	Silver City
Packsaddle	Johnsondale
Parker Peak	California Hot Springs
Peyrone	Sentinel Peak, Solo Peak
Pine Ridge	Giant Forest
Placer County	Greek Store
Red Hill	Sentinel Peak, Solo Peak
Redwood Mountain	General Grant Grove
Redwood Meadow	Lodgepole, Triple Divide Peak
Sequoia Creek	General Grant Grove
Silver Creek	Camp Wishon, Moses Mountain
Skagway	Giant Forest
South Peyrone	Sentinel Peak
South Calaveras	Board's Crossing, Crandall Peak, Stanislaus
South Fork	Moses Mountain
Starvation Creek	Johnsondale, California Hot Springs
Surprise	Case Mountain (the grove), Dennison Peak (the vicinity)
Suwanee	Giant Forest
Tuolumne	Anderson Mountain
Wishon	Camp Wishon

PUBLIC AGENCY INFORMATION SOURCES

Visitors should always contact the local grove managing agency to verify current access conditions on dirt roads or other roads subject to seasonal or administrative closures. In the National Forests, district ranger staff usually have the most current information on road conditions in their areas.

Agency information sources for the most commonly visited grove destinations

Calaveras Big Trees State Park: 209-795-2334, P.O. Box 120, Arnold, CA 95223, www.sierra.parks.state.ca.us/cbt.cbt.htm

Sequoia-Kings Canyon National Parks: Ash Mountain Headquarters: Trail information: 559-565-3776, General information 559-565-3341, 47050 Generals Highway, Three Rivers, CA 93271, www.nps.gov/seki

Sequoia National Forest
Headquarters: 559-784-1500, 900 West Grand Avenue, Porterville, CA 93257, www.r5.fs.us/sequoia
Hume Ranger District: 559-338-2251, 35860 E. Kings Canyon Road, Dunlap, CA 93621
Tule Ranger District: 559-539-2607, 32588 Highway 190, Springville, CA 93265
Hot Springs Ranger District: 661-548-6503, Route 4, Box 548, 43474 Parker Pass Drive, California Hot Springs, CA 93207

Yosemite National Park: 209-372-0265, Yosemite National Park, CA 95389, www.nps.gov/yose

Agency information sources on other grove destinations

Mountain Home State Forest: 559-539-2321 P.O. Box 517, Springville, CA 93265. Call 559-539-2855 during months of winter closure

Sierra National Forest
Headquarters: 559-487-5155, 1600 Tollhouse Road, Clovis, CA 93612, www.r5.fs.us/sierra
Mariposa Ranger District (regarding Nelder Grove): 559-683-4665, 41969 Highway 41, Oakhurst, CA 93644
Kings River Ranger District (regarding McKinley Grove): 559-855-8321 (all year) 34849 Maxon Road, Sanger CA 93657 or (summer only) Dinkey Ranger Station, 559-841-3404, Dinkey Route, Shaver Lake, CA 93664

Tahoe National Forest (regarding Placer County Grove): Foresthill Ranger District: 916-376-2224, 22830 Foresthill Road, Foresthill, CA 95631

This section describes the routes to the sequoia groves by geographic region. Because of space limitations and the complexity of access to many groves, it provides only basic directions with limited detail. Remember that access conditions to many groves may change at any time, particularly due to road closures and lack of road maintenance. When in doubt, check on current access conditions with the local park or forest service district office. Trails are not maintained in most of the groves. Only persons with adequate physical fitness and skills should hike to and within groves, particularly cross-country.

I. Northern Sierra Groves

*North Calaveras Grove (Take State Park exit on Highway 4.)

South Calaveras Grove (Take State Park exit on Highway 4, then paved State Park Road, and then trail.)

*Mariposa Grove (From Highway 41, take paved road east to the grove.)

*McKinley Grove (From Highway 168, take paved McKinley Grove Road to the grove.)

Merced Grove (From Highway 120, hike west on closed dirt road.)

Nelder Grove (From Highway 41, take Sugar Pine turnoff, then paved Sky Ranch Road, and then gravel road 6S90.)

*Placer County Grove (From Highway 80, take paved Forest Hill Road, then a short paved road to the grove.)

Tuolumne Grove (From Highway 120, hike on closed paved road.)

II. Kings River Groves

Bearskin Grove (From Highway 180 or 198, take paved Tenmile Creek Road 13S09, and then short dirt road 13S02.)

*Big Stump Grove (on Highway 180)

Boulder Creek Grove (From Highway 198, take paved road 14S02, and then paved road 13S23.)

Cherry Gap Grove (From Highway 180 west of the park entrance, take road 13S97, and then road 13S58. Alternately, from Highway 180, take dirt road 13S03 west at Cherry Gap, and then road 13S58.)

Converse Basin Grove (From Highway 180, take dirt roads 13S03 or 13S55.)

* Denotes an "easily accessible grove"

Evans Grove (From Highway 180 or 198, take paved Tenmile Creek Road 13S09, and then dirt road 13S05 until it is undriveable. Then hike on it. Alternately, from Highway 198 take road 14S02, then road 13S26, then road 13S25, and then trail.)

*Grant Grove** (short paved road west from Highway 180)

*Indian Basin Grove** (on Highway 180)

Kennedy Grove (From Highway 198, take paved road 14S02, then hike on unmaintained dirt road 13S53 at junction of roads 14S02 and 13S23, then cross-country in the grove. Alternately, from paved road 14S02, take dirt road 13S25 to the nearest point to the grove, and then hike cross-country.)

Landslide Grove (From Highway 180 or 198, take paved Tenmile Creek Road 13S09, then hike on closed dirt road 13S33. Alternately, from Highway 198, take road 14S02, and then hike on closed dirt road 14S02C.)

Little Boulder Creek Grove (From Highway 198, take paved road 14S02, then hike on unmaintained dirt road 13S53 at junction of roads 14S02 and 13S23.)

Lockwood Grove (From Highway 180 or 198, take paved Tenmile Creek Road 13S09, and then dirt road 13S05.)

Sequoia Creek Grove (trail from Highway 180)

WILDERNESS CONDITION GROVES

Agnew Grove (From Highway 198, take paved road 14S11, then dirt road 13S11 to the end, then trail, and then travel cross-country to the grove.)

Deer Meadow Grove (From Highway 198, take paved road 14S11, then dirt road 13S11 to the end, then trail, and then travel cross-country to the grove.)

Monarch Grove (From Highway 198, take paved road 14S11, then dirt road 13S11 to the end, then trail, and then travel cross-country to the grove.)

III. Kaweah River Groves

Atwell-East Fork Grove (Atwell and Redwood Creek units) (From Highway 198, take the paved Mineral King Road. Though on a road, most of the grove is in wilderness condition.)

Case Mountain Grove (Off Highway 198, a long dirt road goes to the grove, but public access by vehicle is currently restricted. Inquire with the BLM office.)

*Giant Forest** (On Highway 198. Paved Crescent Meadow-Moro Rock road is within the grove.)

*Lost Grove (on Highway 198)

Redwood Mountain Grove (From Highway 198, take dirt road west through the grove to the Redwood Saddle trailhead. Most of the grove is in wilderness condition.)

WILDERNESS CONDITION GROVES

Atwell-East Fork Grove (East Fork section) (From Highway 198, take the paved Mineral King Road, and then trail south from the Atwell Mill trailhead.)

Board Camp Grove (From Highway 198, take the paved South Fork Road, the often unmaintained South Fork trail, and then go cross-country.)

Cahoon Creek Grove (From Highway 198, take the paved Mineral King Road, then long trail from the Atwell Mill trailhead to near the lookout above Cahoon Meadow, then cross-country descent to Cahoon Meadow and the grove.)

Castle Creek Grove (From Giant Forest on Highway 198, take the Middle Fork trail, and then difficult cross-country travel across the Middle Fork, *in low water only*, and up Castle Creek. Alternately, from Highway 198 take the paved Mineral King Road, the Atwell trail, the Paradise Ridge trail, and then cross-country descent to the grove.)

Coffeepot Canyon Grove (From Highway 198, take the paved Mineral King Road to Lookout Point, then difficult cross-country travel to the grove—across the East Fork of the Kaweah *in low water only*.)

Eden Creek Grove (From Highway 198, take the paved Mineral King Road, then long trail from Atwell Mill trail-head to the lookout above Cahoon Meadow, then difficult cross-country descent to Cahoon Meadow and the grove. Alternately, from the Mineral King Road, there is very difficult cross-country access across the East Fork of the Kaweah, *in low water only*, and then up Eden Creek.)

Garfield section of Garfield-Dillonwood Grove (From Highway 198, take the paved South Fork Road, and then trail.)

Homers Nose Grove (From Highway 198, take the paved South Fork Road, the often unmaintained South Fork trail, and then go by unmaintained trail or cross-country to the grove.)

Horse Creek Grove (From Highway 198, take the paved Mineral King Road, then long trail from the Atwell Mill trailhead to near the lookout above Cahoon Meadow, then cross-country descent to Cahoon Meadow and the grove.)

Muir Grove (From Dorst Campground off Highway 198, take trail.)

New Oriole Grove (From Highway 198, take the paved Mineral King Road, then the Squirrel Creek dirt road, and then go cross-country to the grove.)

Oriole Grove (From Highway 198, take the paved Mineral King Road, then the Squirrel Creek dirt road, and then go cross-country to the grove. Alternately, from the Mineral King Road go on trails or unmaintained trails to the upper Atwell section of Atwell-East Fork Grove, and then cross-country.)

Pine Ridge Grove (From Dorst Campground off Highway 198, take trail to Muir Grove, and then difficult cross-country travel.)

Redwood Meadow Grove (From Giant Forest on Highway 198, take the Middle Fork trail and the Cliff Creek trail. Alternately, a longer access is From Highway 198, to the paved Mineral King Road, then trail north from Atwell Mill trailhead.)

Skagway Grove (From Dorst Campground off Highway 198, take trail to Muir Grove, and then difficult cross-country travel.)

South Fork Grove (From Highway 198, take the paved South Fork Road, the often unmaintained South Fork trail, and then cross-country to the grove.)

Surprise Grove (From Highway 198, take the paved South Fork Road, the South Fork trail to near Clough Cave, and then difficult cross-country travel.)

Suwanee Grove (From Highway 198, go cross-country to the grove.)

IV. The Other Southern Sierra Groves

*Alder Creek Grove** (From Highway 190, take road 216 north to the Sequoia Crest development and the grove.)

Black Mountain Grove (From Highway 190, take the Coy Flat turnoff at Camp Nelson and then go south on dirt road 21S94 to the grove. Alternately, from Western Divide Highway SM107, turn west on road 21S94 near Nobe Young Creek, and continue to the grove.)

Cunningham Grove (From Western Divide Highway SM107, take dirt road 22S08, or hike on closed sections of the road and then go cross-country to the grove.)

Deer Creek Grove (From near the junction of paved roads SM50 and SM56 at the Hot Springs Ranger Station, take road 23S04 to the lower or upper grove.)

Dillonwood section of Garfield-Dillonwood Grove (Public access on dirt road currently restricted due to private property. Inquire with Sequoia National Forest.)

Freeman Creek Grove (From Highway 190 near Quaking Aspen, take a short dirt road north to the trailhead above the grove, then trail. Alternately, from Western Divide Highway SM107, take paved road SM50 or dirt road 22S02 to paved road 22S82, then north on 22S82, and then by trail or cross-country into the lower grove. Most of the grove interior is in wilderness condition.)

*Long Meadow Grove (on Western Divide Highway SM107)

*McIntyre Grove (From Highway 190, take the short road to the Belknap campground area. Most of this large grove is in wilderness condition.)

*Mountain Home Grove (From Highway 198, take paved Road 220. Alternately, take paved Road 296 from Highway 190. There are several dirt roads within the grove, including the dirt River Road to the canyon part of the grove. The upper canyon section of the grove is in wilderness condition.)

North Cold Spring Grove (Public access on dirt roads is currently restricted. Inquire at the Tule River Indian Reservation headquarters.)

Packsaddle Grove (From Western Divide Highway SM107, take paved road SM50, and then dirt road 23S64 to the edge of the grove. The grove interior is in wilderness condition.)

Parker Peak Grove (Public access on dirt roads is currently restricted. Inquire at the Tule River Indian Reservation headquarters.)

Peyrone Grove (From Highway 190, take the Coy Flat turnoff at Camp Nelson and then go south on dirt road 21S94 to near the grove. Alternately, from Western Divide Highway SM107, turn west on Road 21S94 near Nobe Young Creek. From Road 21S94, above the grove, hike down on closed dirt roads to the grove.)

Red Hill Grove (From Highway 190, take the Coy Flat turnoff at Camp Nelson, and then go south on dirt road 21S94 to the grove. Alternately, from Western Divide Highway SM107, turn west on road 21S94 near Nobe Young Creek.)

South Peyrone Grove (From Highway 190, take the Coy Flat turnoff at Camp Nelson and then go south on dirt road 21S94 to near the grove. Alternately, from Western Divide Highway SM107, turn west on road 21S94 near Nobe Young Creek. From road 21S94, it is a difficult cross-country hike to the grove.)

Starvation Creek Grove (From Highway 190, take paved road SM107, go east on paved road SM50, then take dirt road 23S64, then hike west on a closed section of road 23S64. Alternately, from road SM107, continue west on road SM50, then take road 23S68, or hike on a closed section of that road.)

WILDERNESS CONDITION GROVES

Burro Creek Grove (From a trailhead near the end of the River Road through Mountain Home Grove [see above, p. 117], take the Griswold trail, and then reach the grove by difficult cross-country travel.)

Dennison Grove (From Highway 190, take road 296, then road 276, and then very difficult cross-country access from near Kramer Creek.)

Devils Canyon Grove (From Highway 190, take road 296, then road 276, and then very difficult cross-country access from near Kramer Creek.)

Maggie Mountain Grove (From a trailhead near the end of the River Road through Mountain Home Grove [see above, p. 117], take the Griswold trail and then ascend cross-country in upper Galena Creek to the grove.)

Silver Creek Grove (Hike on the closed extension of the River Road through Mountain Home Grove [see above, p. 117], to near Silver Creek, then trail, and then cross-country within most of the grove.)

Wishon Grove (From Highway 190, take Road 208 to Doyle Springs, and then trail north along the Wishon Fork of the Tule River. Alternately, from Mountain Home Grove [see above, p. 117], take trail south along the Wishon Fork of the Tule River.)

Dilsaver, Lary M., and William C. Tweed. *Challenge of the Big Trees—A Resource History of Sequoia and Kings Canyon National Parks.* Three Rivers, CA: Sequoia Natural History Association, 1990.

Engbeck, Joseph H., Jr. *The Enduring Giants.* Berkeley: University Extension, University of California, 1973.

Flint, Wendell. *To Find the Biggest Tree.* Three Rivers, CA: Sequoia Natural History Association, 1987.

Gillmore, Robert. *Great Walks of Sequoia and Kings Canyon National Parks.* Goffstown, NH: Great Walks Press, 1994.

Gillmore, Robert. *Great Walks Yosemite National Park.* Goffstown, NH: Great Walks Press, 1993.

Johnston, Hank. *They Felled the Redwoods: A Saga of Flumes and Rails in the High Sierra.* Glendale: Trans-Anglo Books, 1983.

Krist, John. *Fifty Best Short Hikes in Yosemite and Sequoia National Parks.* Berkeley: Wilderness Press, 1993.

Muir, John. *The Mountains of California.* Garden City, NY: Doubleday & Company, 1961.

Muir, John. *The Yosemite.* Garden City, NY: Doubleday & Company, 1962.

Proceedings of the Symposium on Giant Sequoias: Their Place in the Ecosystem and Society. Albany CA: Pacific Southwest Research Station, 1992.

Sorensen, Steve. *Day Hiking Sequoia.* 2d ed. Three Rivers, CA: Fuyu Press, 1996.

Willard, Dwight. *Giant Sequoia Groves of the Sierra Nevada: A Reference Guide.* 2d ed. Berkeley, CA: Dwight Willard, 1995.

PHOTO CREDITS

Abbott Creek, 40, 44
Abbott Creek Grove, 40, 44
Adam Tree (Mountain Home Grove), 92
Agassiz Tree (South Calaveras Grove), 18
Agnew Grove, 56, 57, 114
Alder Creek
    South Fork, 95
Alder Creek Grove, 65, 95-96, 99, 116
Alerce Tree, 45
American River, 15, 73
Atwell-East Fork Grove, 77-80, 114, 115
Atwell Grove, 77
Atwell Mill, 79
Atwell Mill Campground, 79
Atwell Trailhead, 74
Auto Log (Giant Forest), 71

Balch Park, 89, 90, 93
Balch Park Campground, 90
Balch Park Road, 90
Barton Flat Creek, 48
Bear Creek, 89, 96
Bear Creek Road, 90
Bear Creek Trail, 96
Bearskin Grove, 46-47, 113
Beetle Rock, 71
Belknap Campground (McIntyre Grove), 96
Big Baldy, 62
Big Oak Flat Road, 18, 19
Big Stump (North Calaveras Grove), 16
Big Stump Grove, 40-41, 113
Big Tree Creek, 43
Big Trees Creek, 17
Big Trees Lodge (Mariposa Grove), 22
Black Mountain Beauty, 97, 99
Black Mountain Grove, 97, 99, 100, 101, 116
Black Mountain Ridge, 99
Board Camp Grove, 80, 81, 115
Boole Tree (Converse Basin Grove), 31, 32, 33, 34,
    92, 95
Boulder Creek, 53, 55, 56, 57
Boulder Creek Canyon, 50, 53, 57
Boulder Creek Grove, 55-56, 113
Bristlecone Pine, 45
Bull Buck Tree (Nelder Grove), 25, 26, 97
Bureau of Land Management, 65, 74, 75
Burnt Monarch (Big Stump Grove), 40, 41
Burro Creek, 95
Burro Creek Grove, 94-95, 118

Cabin Creek, 31, 34
Cabin Creek Grove, 31

Cahoon Creek Grove, 77, 115
Calaveras Big Trees State Park, 15, 17, 65
Calaveras Groves. *See* North Calaveras Grove; South
    Calaveras Grove
California Institute of Technology, 26
California Tree (Grant Grove), 43
California Tree (Mariposa Grove), 20
Camp Lena, 92
Camp Nelson, 95, 96
Camp 3 (Converse Basin Grove), 35
Camp 4 Grove, 48
Camp 7 (Evans Grove), 52
Carr Wilson Grove, 96
Case Mountain Grove, 74-75, 114
Castle Creek Grove, 72, 115
Castro Tree (Freeman Creek Grove), 105
Cedar Creek, 101
Centennial Stump (Grant Grove), 43
Centennial Tree (Mountain Home Grove), 93
Chase, Joseph Smeaton, 51
Cherry Gap Grove, 35, 39-40, 113
Chicago Stump (Converse Basin Grove), 32
Circle Meadow, 70, 71
Clark, Galen, 22
Coast Redwood, 83
Coffeepot Canyon Grove, 81, 115
Colony Mill, 79
Comb Spur, 31
Comstock Mill, 40, 41
Condor Nest Tree (Starvation Creek Grove), 109
Congress Trail (Giant Forest), 70
Converse Basin, 26, 34, 31-33, 34, 35-37, 49, 50, 64
Converse Basin Grove, 27, 31-33, 34, 35-37, 38, 39,
    45, 52, 69, 113
Converse Basin Mill, 35. *See* also Converse Mill
Converse Creek, 31, 36
Converse Mill, 35, 36-37, 39
Converse Mountain, 31, 37
Coulterville Road, 19
Coy Flat Road, 96
Crane Creek. *See* North Crane Creek
Crawford Road, 99
Crescent Meadow, 69, 71
Cunningham Grove, 106, 108, 116

Day Tree (Alder Creek Grove), 95
Dead Giant (Grant Grove), 44
Dead Giant (Tuolumne Grove), 18, 19
Deadman Creek, 99
Deer Creek Grove, 73, 109, 116
Deer Meadow Grove, 56-57, 114
Deer Meadow Ridge Trail, 56, 57

Dennison Grove, 81-82, 118
Dennison Ridge, 85
Devils Canyon Grove, 81-82, 118
Dillon Mill, 84
Dillon, Nathan, 84
Dillonwood Grove, 65, 82, 84-85, 117
Discovery Tree (North Calaveras Grove), 16
Dogwood, 74, 75
Dogwood Meadow, 90, 91, 92
Dorst Campground, 66
Dowd, A. T., 19

East Fork Grove, 77, 79, 80
Eden Creek Grove, 76, 77, 115
Ella Falls, 46
Empire State Tree (North Calaveras Grove), 17
Enterprise Mill, 93
Euclid Tree (Mountain Home Grove), 92
Evans Creek, 50, 52
Evans Grove, 34, 38, 48, 49-50, 52-53, 56, 64, 114

Flint, Wendell, 20, 32, 62, 79, 92, 97, 98
Forest King (Nelder Grove), 26
Founders Group (Giant Forest), 70
Franklin Tree (Giant Forest), 69
Frasier Mill Campground, 90, 92
Freeman Creek, 105, 106
Freeman Creek Grove, 105-06, 117

Galena Creek, 89, 94
Garfield-Dillonwood Grove, 65, 82, 84-85, 115
General Grant Grove. See Grant Grove
General Grant National Park, 43
General Grant Tree (Grant Grove), 42, 43, 69, 70
General Lee Tree (Grant Grove), 43
General Lee Tree (Packsaddle Grove), 108
General Noble Tree (Converse Basin Grove), 32
General Sherman Tree (Giant Forest), 20, 26, 32, 43,
   68, 69, 70, 95, 98
General's Highway, 69
Genesis Tree (Mountain Home Grove), 90, 92
Ghost Tree (Packsaddle Grove), 108
Giant Forest, 17, 32, 43, 50, 61, 68-72, 79, 84, 92,
   96, 98, 112, 114
Giant Sequoia National Monument, 7, 17, 65, 97,
   108, 109
Gigantea Campground (McKinley Grove), 27
Golden Trout Wilderness, 89, 106
Goodmill Creek, 35, 39
Goshawk Tree (Freeman Creek Grove), 105
Grant Grove, 40, 41-44, 70, 114
Grant Tree. See General Grant Tree
Grizzly Giant (Mariposa Grove), 20, 22

Hart Tree (Redwood Mountain Grove), 62
Hedrick Mill, 92
Hidden Falls River Road, 89
Hoist Ridge, 31, 35, 36, 37, 39
Homers Nose Grove, 80-81, 115
Homers Nose Tree, 81
Horse Creek, 77
Horse Creek Grove, 77, 115
Horseshoe Bend Grove, 50
House Group (Giant Forest), 70
Huckleberry Meadow, 71
Hume Lake, 37, 47, 48, 52, 53, 56
Hume Lake Mill, 46, 48, 49, 52
Hume Ranger District, 57
Hume, Thomas, 36
Hume-Bennett Lumber Company, 37, 48, 49, 52, 53
Huntington, Ellsworth, 38, 84, 93
Hyde's Mill, 64

Indian Basin Grove, 37-38, 114
Indian Creek, 38
Indian Meadow, 38
Ishi Giant (Kennedy Grove), 53

Kaweah River, 82
   East Fork, 76, 77
   Marble Fork, 68, 69
   Middle Fork, 68, 71, 72, 74
   South Fork, 80, 81, 82, 85
Kennedy Grove, 53-54, 55, 56, 114
Kennedy Meadow Creek, 53
King Arthur Tree (Garfield-Dillonwood Grove), 84
King of the Forest (Tuolumne Grove), 18
Kings Canyon, 27, 31, 32, 36, 37, 47, 49, 50, 52, 54,
   56, 57
Kings Canyon National Park, 39, 40, 41, 44, 46, 61,
   62, 69, 77
Kings River, 17, 20, 25, 26, 47, 56, 57, 73
Kings River Lumber Company, 35, 36, 39

Landslide Grove, 46-47, 114
Leonard, Zenas, 18, 19
Lincoln Tree (Giant Forest), 70, 72
Lincoln Tree (Grant Grove), 43
Little Boulder Creek Grove, 53, 55, 56, 114
Little Redwood Meadow, 74
Lloyd Meadow Creek, 106
Lockwood Creek, 47, 49
Lockwood Grove, 47-49, 52, 114
Log Meadow, 71
Long Canyon Creek, 99
Long Meadow Grove, 106, 117
Lost Grove, 66, 115

Maggie Mountain Grove, 94, 118
Mariposa Grove, 20-22, 23, 25, 26, 76, 85, 113
Mariposa Grove Museum, 21
Mark Twain Tree (Big Stump Grove), 41
Massachusetts Tree (Mariposa Grove), 22
McGee Fire (Converse Basin Grove), 37, 39
McIntyre Grove, 96-97, 117
McKinley Grove, 27, 113
McKinley Grove Road, 27
Merced Grove, 18-19, 113
Methuselah Tree (Mountain Home Grove), 90, 92
Middle Tule Grove, 89
Millwood, 35, 36, 37, 39, 40, 52
Millwood Mill, 36
Mineral King Road, 76, 80
Monarch Divide, 38, 49
Monarch Grove, 56, 57, 114
Monarch Wilderness Area, 50, 53
Moro Rock, 69, 71
Moses Gulch, 89, 90, 92
Moses Mountain, 89
Moses Mountain Grove, 89
Moss Creek, 19
Mother of the Forest (North Calaveras Grove), 15, 16
Mountain Aire, 99
Mountain Home Grove, 32, 34, 50, 84, 89-94,
  95, 117
Mountain Home State Forest, 65, 89, 90
Muir Grove, 66, 67, 75, 116
Muir, John, 21, 25, 32, 43, 44, 51, 64, 89
Muir Snag (Converse Basin Grove), 32, 45

Needles, The, 105
Needles Trail, 106
Nelder Basin, 25, 26
Nelder Grove, 25-26, 27, 34, 97, 113
Nelder Tree, 26
New Oriole Grove, 75-76, 116
North Calaveras Grove, 15-16, 17, 19, 22, 73,
  76, 113
North Cold Spring Grove, 101, 117
North Crane Creek, 18
North Grove Trail Loop (Grant Grove), 44

Old Adam (Big Stump Grove), 40
Old Goliath (South Calaveras Grove), 18
Old One Hundred (Giant Forest), 70
Olmsted, Frederick Law, Jr., 17
Oregon Tree (Grant Grove), 43
Oriole Grove, 75-76, 116

Packsaddle Giant, 108
Packsaddle Grove, 108, 117
Palace Hotel Tree (South Calaveras Grove), 17
Parker Peak Grove, 101, 117
Patriarch Tree (McIntyre Grove), 96
Peyrone Grove, 100-01, 117
Pierce Fire, 62, 64
Pine Ridge Grove, 67-68, 116
Pinus longaeva, 45
Pioneer Cabin Tree (North Calaveras Grove), 16
Placer County Grove, 15, 73, 109, 113
President Tree (Giant Forest), 70
Princess Campground (Indian Basin Grove), 38

Quaking Aspen Campground (McIntyre Grove), 96

Rancheria Creek, 89, 92
Rattlesnake Creek, 57
Red Hill Grove, 100, 101, 117
Redwood Canyon, 61
Redwood Creek, 49, 50, 61, 62
  East Fork, 62
Redwood Creek Grove, 77, 79
Redwood Crossing, 89, 92
Redwood Meadow Campground, 106
Redwood Meadow Grove, 74, 116
Redwood Mountain Grove, 34, 61-64, 69, 70, 77,
  79, 115
Redwood Mountain Ridge, 62
Redwood Saddle, 61
River Road, 90
Roosevelt, Theodore, 21
Roosevelt Tree (Redwood Mountain Grove), 61, 62
Rouch Mill, 92
Round Meadow, 71
Rundel, Philip, 62, 70

Sanger Company, 36, 37
Sanger Lumber Company, 37, 52, 53
Senate Group (Giant Forest), 70
Sequoia Creek, 46
Sequoia Creek Grove, 44, 46, 114
Sequoia Crest, 95
Sequoia Lake, 46
Sequoia National Forest, 17, 31, 37, 39, 40, 41, 43,
  46, 47, 49, 53, 55, 56, 57, 61, 64, 65, 82, 84, 89,
  94, 95, 96, 97, 100, 101, 105, 106, 108, 109
Sequoia National Park, 17, 19, 20, 47, 66, 67, 68, 72,
  74, 75, 76, 77, 79, 80, 81, 82, 85
Sequoia Railroad, 35, 36, 39, 40
Sequoia sempervirens, 83
Shake Camp, 90, 93
Shaver Lake, 27
Siamese Twins (Tuolumne Grove), 18

Sierra National Forest, 25, 27
Silver Creek, 94
Silver Creek Grove, 90, 94, 118
Skagway Grove, 67-68, 116
Slate Mountain, 96
Slate Mountain Roadless Area, 97
Snowslide Canyon, 85
Soldiers' Trail Tree (Giant Forest), 70
South Calaveras Grove, 17-18, 66, 113
South Fork Grove, 81, 116
South Fork Road, 82
South Peyrone Grove, 101, 117
Spanish Mountain, 47
Squirrel Creek, 76
Stagg Tree (Alder Creek Grove), 65, 92, 95
Stanislaus River
    North Fork, 17
Starvation Creek Grove, 108, 109, 118
Stump Meadow (Converse Basin Grove), 34, 35, 36
Sudworth, George, 74
Sugar Bowl, 62
Sugar Bowl Grove, 62
Summit Road, 90
Summit Tree (Mountain Home Grove), 92
Sunset Rock, 71
Surprise Grove, 81, 116
Suwanee Grove, 68, 75, 116

Table Mountain Ridge, 106
Tahoe National Forest, 15
Tehipite Dome, 50
Telescope Tree (Freeman Creek Grove), 105
Tenmile Creek, 46, 52
Tharp, Hale, 71
Tioga Road, 18
Trail of 100 Giants, 106
Tree-Naming, 23
Tulare County, 65, 89
Tule Indian Reservation, 65, 97, 100, 101
Tule River
    Middle Fork, 96, 99
    North Fork, 82, 89
    North Fork of Middle Fork, 89, 94, 95
    South Fork, 97, 100
    South Fork of Middle Fork, 97
    Wishon Fork. *See* North Fork of Middle Fork
Tunnel Log (Giant Forest), 71
Tuolumne Grove, 18-19, 113
Twain, Mark, Tree. *See* Mark Twain Tree

University of California, 34, 61, 64, 65
Upper Abbott Mill, 39
Upper Nelder Creek, 25

Verplank Creek, 31

Walker, Joseph, Party, 18, 19
Washington Tree (Giant Forest), 43, 70, 98
Washington Tree (Mariposa Grove), 20, 26
Wawona Road, 20
Wawona (Tunnel) Tree, 16, 20
Weed, C. L., 22
Wheeler Peak (Nevada), 46
Whitaker Forest, 34, 61, 62, 64
Whitaker, Horace, 64
Wilson Creek, 99
    West Fork, 99
Windy Cliffs, 50
Windy Creek, 100
Windy Gulch, 50, 52
Windy Gulch Basin, 50
Wishon Grove, 94-95, 118
Wuksachi Village, 71

Yosemite National Park, 16, 18, 19, 20, 22, 25, 65, 85
Yosemite Valley, 22